NOT HEARERS ONLY
VOLUME IV

Bible Studies in the Epistle of James

JOHN BLANCHARD

WORD BOOKS
LONDON

Acknowledgement is made to The Division of
Christian Education of the National Council
of Churches of Christ for quotations from
The Revised Standard Version of the Bible,
Copyright © 1946 and 1952.

Published by Word Books, London, a
Division of Word (UK) Ltd., Park Lane,
Hemel Hempstead, Hertfordshire.

ISBN 0 85009 047 4

Made and printed in Great Britain by
Hunt Barnard Printing Ltd.,
Aylesbury, Bucks.

TO JOYCE

By the same author:

NOT HEARERS ONLY: VOLUME I
NOT HEARERS ONLY: VOLUME II
NOT HEARERS ONLY: VOLUME III
RIGHT WITH GOD
READ MARK LEARN

CONTENTS

FOREWORD

I have thoroughly enjoyed reading this volume of John Blanchard's Commentary. It is certainly fully up to the standard of his earlier volumes. Mr Blanchard has the facility for dealing with the text adequately, but always in such a way as to compel attention. While he claims not to deal with technical matters, his treatment of the text shows he is not unaware of such issues, and there is certainly no trace of superficiality in his work.

I have always found the Letter of James particularly challenging, and have given Bible Readings on this book at Conventions. Nevertheless, I felt on taking up Mr Blanchard's book I just had to read on, and I was truly inspired by what I read. He has a flair for putting things succinctly and for producing apt illustrations. May God use this volume to awaken His people in this modern age of materialism to some of the implications of living the Christian life in an affluent society. Readers will, I feel sure, be greatly helped by the balanced approach of the author to such controversial issues as that of healing. It is good to read a commentary which gives the impression that it has been written neither to display scholastic brilliance, nor to score points for a particular interpretation, but simply to help the reader enter more fully into the true meaning of God's Word.

Rev. GILBERT W. KIRBY.

PREFACE

The Epistle of James has always had a peculiar fascination for me, ever since I first 'discovered' it soon after my conversion. From then on I have been drawn to it again and again. It was one of the first parts of the Bible I went through as a Bible Class leader at Holy Trinity Church, Guernsey in 1958, using, I remember, Canon Guy King's book 'A Belief that Behaves' as a general basis. Later, when I travelled to England as a member of a parish mission team, the Vicar of the Church involved based his daily ministry to the team on the same Epistle, and I began to gain new insights into this great little book.

Some years afterwards, as a staff evangelist with the National Young Life Campaign, I dug a little deeper as I studied it in series with several NYLC branches in the West Country. Then in 1966, on the staff of the Movement for World Evangelization, I led what has since become a large number of delightfully happy house-parties in Europe and elsewhere. Yet again I felt irresistibly drawn to the Epistle of James as a basis for the morning Bible Hour, and I found myself returning to the text with a new enthusiasm to discover fresh truths from the familiar words.

In the Autumn of 1968 I accepted an invitation to write a series of Bible Studies for *Sunday Companion*, and found great joy in re-shaping material on the first chapter of James to meet the particular demands of 1,000-word articles for 29 weeks. Those articles, later translated for use in Eastern Europe, greatly added to requests I was already receiving to consider producing a devotional study on the whole Epistle of James in more permanent form. In answering those requests, it was initially planned to prepare three volumes, but the third and fourth chapters of James's Epistle were found to contain such a wealth of material that it became necessary to extend the work to four volumes, of which this is the last.

Anyone even vaguely familiar with the New Testament knows the general line of the Epistle of James, and a glance at the titles of books devoted to it confirms the assessment that is made – 'The Behavior of Belief' (Spiros Zodhiates), 'A Belief that Behaves' (Guy H. King), 'Make your Faith Work' (Louis H. Evans), 'Faith that Works' (John L. Bird), 'The Tests of Faith' (J. Alec Motyer). These titles are all trying to crystallise the same truth, that James is a *practical* book, dealing with everyday life for the man in the street. Yet it is not devoid of doctrine, as we shall see when we begin to dig into the text. As Alec Motyer puts it, '. . . the distinctive value of James is his striking grasp of the integration of truth and life.' I agree! – and it is precisely this integration of truth and life that makes James so relevant today. Even as Christians we seem to have an almost incurable tendency to be unbalanced. We either major on accumulating truth, to the neglect of enthusiastic action, or we dash around in a mad whirl of activity, to the neglect of faith and truth. James provides just the balance we need. It is said that when a student was once asked to name his favourite translation of the Bible he replied 'My mother's'. 'Is it a translation into English?', his friend went on. 'No', he replied, 'it is a translation into action!' That, in a nutshell, is James's great concern.

In these studies, I have not sought to deal with critical and technical issues, which are beyond both my aim and my ability. I have therefore assumed, for instance, that the writer of the Epistle was 'James, the Lord's brother' (Galatians 1. 19) and that it was written at sometime between A.D. 45 and A.D. 62. I have simply come to the Word of God with an open heart and sought the Holy Spirit's help in understanding and applying it. In preparing these studies for publication in this form, I have sought, by use of the second person, to retain as much as possible of the personal thrust of the spoken word.

I would like to repeat my thanks to the Council of the Movement for World Evangelization for the privilege of serving the Movement in the ministry of the Word of God, and to Word (UK) Limited for their kind offer to publish these studies. My warm thanks are also due to The Rev. Gilbert Kirby, who graciously found time to read the manuscript and write the Foreword to this particular volume. Finally, I owe an immense debt of gratitude to Miss Sheila Hellberg, who has typed and re-typed every word of all four volumes. The quality of her work has been excellent, and her patience proverbial!

My prayer for this fourth volume remains the same as for the three that preceded it, that the Lord will help writer and reader alike to obey His own clear command, given through James, to be 'doers of the word, and *not hearers only*'!

Croydon, Surrey.
March, 1974.   JOHN BLANCHARD.

Chapter 1

THE MADNESS OF MATERIALISM

'Go to now, ye rich men, weep and howl for your miseries that shall come upon you.

Your riches are corrupted, and your garments are moth-eaten.

Your gold and silver is cankered; and the rust of them shall be a witness against you, and shall eat your flesh as it were fire. Ye have heaped treasure together for the last days.

Behold, the hire of the labourers who have reaped down your fields, which is of you kept back by fraud, crieth: and the cries of them which have reaped are entered into the ears of the Lord of Sabaoth.

Ye have lived in pleasure on the earth, and been wanton; ye have nourished your hearts, as in a day of slaughter.

Ye have condemned and killed the just; and he doth not resist you.'

(James 5:1–6)

Most Christians may feel that they can 'switch off' after the first six words of this passage! 'Go to now, ye rich men', says James – but most people within the church would claim that they were not rich. On reading through the remainder of the passage, they might also feel that it misses them for another reason, namely that these verses seem to have been written to people who were not Christians. That is a fairly safe assumption in view of the behaviour of these people, as we will notice in detail later.

So, within the church, one could understand the reaction
of a person without a deep understanding of the Word of
God saying 'This has got nothing to do with me. After
all, I am a Christian, and this is written to unbelievers. I
am not a rich man and this is specifically written to rich
men'. However, there is a principle that must always
govern our reading of the scriptures, and if we remember
this principle, we will not bypass a passage like this. The
principle, very simply, is this: not all scripture is written
to us, but all scripture is written *for* us. Take the words of
Moses, for instance. They were written and spoken *to* the
people of Israel. Now most Christians do not belong to
the ethnic people of Israel, but those words of Moses were
equally written and spoken *for us*. Take Paul's letters to
the Corinthians. We do not live in Corinth, or in the
1st Century, so his letters were not written *to* us – but
they were written *for* us. Likewise this Epistle of James
was originally written to the *diaspora*, the Jews who were
scattered abroad in times of persecution. Now we may be
neither Jews nor scattered abroad in persecution, but who
can doubt that this Epistle was written *for us*? If we apply
that principle to the passage we have in mind here, then
we will not dare to pass it by. It has something to say to
us. As Paul himself put it, quoting David's words in
Psalm 69 as an example, these things 'were written for
our learning' (Romans 15:4).

Let us now turn to the text. What does James say?
Notice first of all

1. *THE WICKEDNESS HE DENOUNCES.* Four things
come to light here –

(1) *Covetousness* – 'Ye have heaped treasure together
for the last days' (v. 3). Weymouth translates it 'you have
hoarded up wealth in the last days', and that exactly
catches the spirit of it, because the words translated

'heaped together treasure' are in fact one Greek word, *thesaurizo*, from which we get our word 'thesaurus', which basically means a collection. That tells us precisely what James is denouncing here. The phrase speaks for itself. It is the spirit bent on hoarding together every penny possible. This heaping together of treasure refers not so much to the size of what was collected, but to the spirit in which it was gathered together.

When Jesus told the parable of the rich fool in Luke 12 (at which we looked in an earlier study), He told it to illustrate the folly of this very thing. You will remember that in the prelude to the story Jesus said 'Take heed, and beware of all covetousness; for a man's life does not consist in the abundance of his possessions' (Luke 12:15 RSV), while He applied it with the words 'So is he who lays up treasure for himself, and is not rich toward God' (Luke 12:21 RSV). Notice the two words that reveal all – *'for himself'*. His motives in his energetic policy of expansion were selfish and covetous, and the Bible teaches that covetousness is a sin. In fact, it uses the remarkable phrase 'covetousness, which is idolatry' (Colossians 3:5). It is the deification of self. If we are laying up treasure for ourselves, then we are being idolatrous. The Bible is so wonderfully balanced here. It nowhere condemns a good business sense, or industry, or hard work. Nowhere in the Bible is wealth condemned as such; but the laying up of treasure for ourselves in a spirit of ruthless greed is something that is spoken against in the strongest terms.

Notice too that James says that it is a laying up of treasure 'for the last days', or, as the Revised Standard Version puts it – 'in the last days'. The scholars are very confused as to the precise meaning of these words, but I think we will be safe to make the obvious general point that their hoarding up of wealth was merely laying up

wealth for a shrinking and uncertain future. Although
the words towards the end of James 4 were directly ad-
dressed to the same group of people, it is interesting to
note that these words come not very long after James's
comment about the brevity of life. It is literally true that
for all men these *are* the last days; after all, the first ones
have already gone! There is no person for whom these are
not the last days. That is tremendously challenging, and
means that James speaks yet again about the stewardship
of all that God has given us. In doing so, covetousness is
the first wickedness that he denounces. Let us beware of
that, in any measure, in our own lives!

(2) *Corruption* – 'Behold, the hire of the labourers who
have reaped down your fields, which is of you kept back
by fraud . . .' (v. 4).

James asks these ungodly, rich and greedy men to take
note of the fact that there are wages that they have kept
back from those they employ to gather in their harvests.
These men were obviously rich landowners, who hired
men to gather in the fruits of the earth, and, having agreed,
it would seem, to pay them a wage for the job, they then
kept back their wages by fraud. They found some way to
avoid their moral responsibility, and, in doing so, they
were in direct contravention of the law of God. The Old
Testament was quite specific on this point – 'You shall
not oppress your neighbour or rob him. The wages of a
hired servant shall not remain with you all night until the
morning' (Leviticus 19:13 RSV); and again, 'You shall
not oppress a hired servant who is poor and needy . . .
you shall give him his hire on the day he earns it . . . '
(Deuteronomy 24:14–15 RSV).

Any Christian involved in business as an employer
should take very serious note of the Bible's insistence on
scrupulous honesty in dealing with an employee. Jesus

said, 'the labourer deserves his wages' (Luke 10:7 RSV).
Paul wrote that even slaves were to be treated 'justly and
fairly' (Colossians 4:1 RSV). There is a deep, searching
need for a rebirth of uncomplicated honesty in our land
today, a liberation from double-thinking into clear, plain,
straightforward, above-board dealing. It is symptomatic
of our age that we have lost that spirit. For the Christian,
honesty is not the best policy – it is the only one. To be
other than honest is to be guilty in some measure of the
sin of corruption.

(3) *Carelessness* – 'Ye have lived in pleasure on the
earth, and been wanton; ye have nourished your hearts,
as in a day of slaughter' (v. 5). The Amplified Bible
translates this 'Here on earth you have abandoned yourselves to soft prodigal living, and to the pleasures of self-
indulgence and self-gratification. You have fattened your
hearts in a day of slaughter'.

From that amplified translation let me pick out the two
words 'abandoned yourselves'. These seem to take us to
the heart of what James is getting at here. These people
were guilty of carelessness. Having swindled the poor in
order to feather their own nests, these men now lived in
idle ease and luxury, utterly careless of the needs of the
rest of the world. Again, that spirit is roundly condemned
in the Bible. Take this word from Amos for instance –
'Woe to those who are at ease in Zion, and to those who
feel secure in the mountain of Samaria, the notable men
of the first of the nations, to whom the house of Israel
come! Pass over to Calneh, and see; and thence go to
Hamath the great; then go down to Gath of the Philis-
tines. Are they better than these kingdoms? Or is their
territory greater than your territory, O you who put
faraway the evil day, and bring near the seat of violence?
Woe to those who lie upon beds of ivory, and stretch

themselves upon their couches, and eat lambs from the
flock, and calves from the midst of the stall; who sing
songs to the sound of the harp, and like David invent for
themselves instruments of music; who drink wine in
bowls, and anoint themselves with the finest oils, but are
not grieved over the ruin of Joseph!' (Amos 6:1–6 RSV).
Selfish, careless, self-gratification is sin. It is interesting,
and strengthening to one's faith to discover the way in
which the Bible so wonderfully holds together in this kind
of teaching. When Paul says in Romans 13:13, 'Let us
walk honestly' (answering exactly to James's first point,
the need not to be corrupted in our dealings), he goes on
to say, 'not in wantonness'. This careless approach to life
is also condemned by Paul in precisely the same breath.
Perhaps there are few of us who feel that today we can
afford to live in luxury, and we may be tempted to think
that this is one of those phrases that hardly applies to us,
and from which we are hard pressed to draw any relevant
lesson. But this spirit of wantonness can so easily creep
in. The man who deals in tens of pounds is in danger of
becoming wanton as soon as he starts dealing in hundreds;
the man who deals in hundreds is tempted to become
wanton as soon as he deals in thousands; and the man
who deals in thousands is in danger as soon as he reaches
tens of thousands. Let us beware! The principle we need
to hold before us is one that was so pithily put by Thomas
Manton – 'God gave us wealth for another purpose than
to spend it in pleasures'. Let us beware in any measure of
that spirit of selfish, careless, self-gratification which encourages the total ignoring of other people's needs.

(4) *Cruelty* – 'Ye have condemned and killed the just;
and he doth not resist you'. Notice the way in which
James's condemnation of these men has built up – covetousness, then corruption, then carelessness, and now

cruelty. This is an interesting verse because some translators and commentators see in the phrase 'the just' the Lord Jesus Himself. If that is so, it is an echo of Peter's words to the crowd in Jerusalem – 'But ye denied the Holy One and the Just, and desired a murderer to be granted unto you; and killed the Prince of life, whom God hath raised from the dead; whereof we are witnesses' (Acts 3:13–15). I am not too impressed with that interpretation, for the simple reason that Jesus was not hounded to death so much by the rich as by the religious, and that because His teaching cut radically across theirs. I think it wiser to assume that James is referring to another tragic truth of human history, and that is that wicked men, when raised to great wealth and power, have again and again persecuted and oppressed the poor, Christians included, even to the point of shedding blood in order to gain their own ends. In the words of Lord Acton's famous aphorism – 'All power corrupts, and absolute power corrupts absolutely'.

This would give our verse an immediate link with chapter 4 verse 2, where James says, 'Ye lust, and have not: ye kill, and desire to have, and cannot obtain: ye fight and war, yet ye have not, because ye ask not'. When we were studying that passage, we referred to one of the historical instances that would spring immediately to the mind of the original hearers of this Epistle, the story of the wicked King Ahab and Naboth's vineyard. Here was a classic example of a man who was covetous, corrupt, careless and cruel, and was even prepared to shed blood in order to satisfy his desires. It is a striking example – but it is certainly not an isolated one. History, before and since, records many who rose to power as cruel, heartless despots.

But we must notice the other phrase, at the end of the

verse – 'he doth not resist you'. A pathetic kind of phrase, this – yet surely this is one of the things that truly qualifies a man to be called 'just'. Going back to the example of the Lord Jesus, we find Peter saying of Him that 'When He was reviled, He did not revile in return; when He suffered, He did not threaten; but He trusted to Him who judges justly' (1 Peter 2:23 RSV). That also reminds us of the Lord's own comment in the Sermon on the Mount – 'Do not resist one who is evil. But if any one smites you on the right cheek, turn to him the other also' (Matthew 5:39 RSV). Have we ever seriously tried to work out the implication of that teaching?

To sum up so far, let us just say this. To oppress any man is sin. Any kind of oppression of our fellow man is sin. We are to treat men with the dignity of their humanity. We are not all the children of God by regeneration, but we are all God's creatures nevertheless, and one of the things that the Bible so challengingly teaches, is that we should treat all of our fellow men regardless of their beliefs or behaviour, with that special dignity that God has put upon them as men. God has separated all men from the rest of His creation, according to His own wisdom, and we are to treat all men in the light of that fact. To oppress any man in any way is sin. How much greater the sin when we bully and batter a man who offers no resistance. On the other hand, when we as Christians are oppressed or wronged, then the right attitude is to follow the example of the Lord Jesus who 'when He was reviled, He did not revile in return'.

Following through this word by James, we have looked at the wickedness he denounces. Now see

2. *THE WARNING HE DELIVERS.*

Like his denunciation, this is scattered throughout the passage, but it is dramatized in the opening verse – 'Weep and howl for your miseries that shall come upon you'. In other words, James is saying that there is trouble ahead for the people who are acting in the way we saw in the earlier part of the study.

The 'miseries' to which he refers are capable of two meanings, both of them true. Firstly, there is the destruction of Jerusalem in A.D. 70, perhaps within 10 years of James writing. The bloody siege led by the Roman General Titus claimed over a million lives, a horrifying figure even in these modern days. In that slaughter, the richest men were those who were the first targets for the looters and murderers. So, in a very vivid way, James could say to these people, 'weep and howl for your miseries that shall come upon you'. He could say truthfully that they were heaping up treasure 'for the last days'.

Secondly, there is the day of judgment. James points out that the miseries of that day are absolutely certain – 'your miseries that *shall* come upon you'. These men had been covetous, corrupt, careless, and cruel. They had lived and worked and spoken and grasped as if there had been no God, no judgment, no heaven and no hell. But the day of judgment was coming. This is the thrust of James's opening verse – 'your miseries . . . shall come upon you'.

The story is told of a godless American farmer who wrote to his local newspaper, 'I have been conducting an experiment with one of my fields. I have ploughed it on a Sunday, I sowed the seed on a Sunday, I irrigated and tended it on a Sunday, I reaped down the harvest on a Sunday – and I want to tell you that this October I have the biggest crop in the whole neighbourhood'. The editor published the letter and he added this footnote – 'God does not settle all His accounts in October'. There is such a thing as judgment to come, and we are going to have

this second meaning in mind as we look at the details of
the 'miseries' mentioned by James. He says, in effect, that
these men will face three things. The first is this –

(1) *Testimony.* The day is coming, says James, when
the impenitent, covetous, rich man will have to listen to
three voices giving testimony –

Firstly, the testimony of ill-gotten gains – 'the hire of
the labourers who have reaped down your fields, which is
of you kept back by fraud, *crieth*' (v. 4). Our vices will
have voices! They will speak, and speak the truth. They
will give evidence against us on that great day. They will
testify in the matter of the condemnation of the ungodly,
and they will testify in the matter of diminution of reward
for the Christian. This is the first voice James mentions.

Secondly, the testimony of those they have defrauded –
'and the cries of them which have reaped are entered into
the ears of the Lord of Sabaoth' (v. 4). The testimony of
those they have defrauded now joins with the testimony
of their ill-gotten gains. The word 'Sabaoth', incidentally,
is an unusual one. It means, 'armies' or 'hosts'. The only
other New Testament use is in Romans 9:29, where Paul
quotes the prophet Isaiah. There are two obvious Biblical
examples of the voices of the wronged crying out, and
those cries entering into the ears of God. God tells the
murderer Cain 'The voice of your brother's blood is crying to me from the ground' (Genesis 4:10 RSV). Cain had
stopped Abel's blood from circulating, but he could not
stop it speaking! What a dramatic illustration of this
truth! Then towards the end of their slavery in Egypt, we
read of the Israelites, 'And the people of Israel groaned
under their bondage, and cried out for help, and their cry
under bondage came up to God' (Exodus 2:23 RSV).
What a terrifying prospect James is predicting for these
rich men! Those they had wronged cried out to God, and

God had heard their cry. He had registered their protest, and one day God would call those same voices to give evidence against these rich men. And this God of judgment, this hearing God, this God who had registered all these protests was the Lord of Hosts – the hosts of heaven, the sun, the moon, the stars, the angelic hosts, and, in fact, all the hosts of the universe. Testimony against them would be given to the One in control of the eternal destinies of all men. What a terrible prospect!

Thirdly, the testimony of their unused possessions – 'The rust of them shall be a witness against you' (v. 3). Here is another voice speaking, and this time it will not be the voice of the wages they kept back from the labourers, not the voice of the people they had defrauded, but the voice of their own rusted possessions that they had not used to the glory of God. This rust would be a voice, a testimony, a witness against them, as James says. While on earth, they had been surrounded by human need, and yet they heaped all this treasure to themselves. One day it would be rusted and useless – and its rust would be vocal!

These three voices make up the first thing these men must face – testimony. The next thing is

(2) *Transformation* – 'Your riches are corrupted, and your garments are moth-eaten, your gold and silver is cankered' (Amplified Bible 'completely rusted through') (vv. 2–3). What a transformation! The things in which they had trusted for status, security and satisfaction, were now absolutely worthless. Their riches were rotten, their clothes were rags, and their silver was rusty. They were all worthless. They had had such plans and visions, they were going to do great things, they were going to heap up more and more, and now it lay worthless at their feet.

As I was preparing this study I read a report in a local

newspaper about three youths who burgled an old woman's cottage. They intended to steal £2,000, but they came away with a cheese sandwich, a 10p piece and a handbag stuffed with newspaper! They were arrested, found guilty, and remanded for sentence at the forth-coming Assize. They had set their eyes on so much, and wound up with so little! The Word of God says that 'riches profit not in the day of wrath' (Proverbs 11:4). People who are setting their eyes on great riches in the here and now will discover them to be worth nothing there and then. This is why I have called this whole study 'The madness of materialism'.

Incidentally, as an illustration of how worthless ma-terial issues are in this context, notice that James des-cribes their gold and silver as 'cankered', or rusted, whereas in fact gold and silver never rust! James is not making a mistake here, he is deliberately using this phrase to show that the very things they thought were imperish-able and unaffected by time, were utterly without worth in eternity. Jeremiah puts it like this – 'Like the partridge that gathers a brood which she did not hatch, so is he who gets riches but not by right; in the midst of his days they will leave him, and at his end he will be a fool' (Jeremiah 17:11 RSV). There will be a transformation, and this will join with the voices of testimony to add to the wicked man's miseries. But that is not all. James adds a third thing –

(3) *Torment* – 'and shall eat your flesh as it were fire' (v. 3). What a fearful word! Yet it is faithful to the truth of scripture, that God is a God of unshakable justice and that the ungodly 'shall be punished with everlasting des-truction from the presence of the Lord, and from the glory of His power' (2 Thessalonians 1:9). The reference to hell is inescapable. Jesus spoke of hell as including 'the

fire that never shall be quenched' (Mark 9:43), while the gentle John spoke twice of the 'lake of fire' (Revelation 20:10 and 14). Eternal, conscious punishment for the ungodly is clearly taught in the Bible.

We have now covered all the words of the text in these opening six verses of James 5. Although they are true, they are in fact entirely negative and speaking only of the ungodly rich. Yet like all scripture, as we saw at the beginning of the study, these things are written for our learning, and I want therefore to add one last and very brief point which must all be filled out by inference.

3. *THE WORTH WE CAN DRAW.* What can we draw from these verses that spoke 2,000 years ago to a group of ungodly and rich men to whom the fall of Jerusalem was about to happen, and who were being warned of their particular torment in the judgment to come? I think there are very positive lessons here for Christians. Let me touch on just four.

(1) There is not a word here against riches as such, but only against the ungodly way in which they were gained and used. The Bible does not say that money is the root of all evil, but that 'the love of money is the root of all evil' (1 Timothy 6:10). The Bible never condemns a man for being wealthy. Abraham was 'very rich in cattle, in silver and in gold' (Genesis 13:2); David died 'in a good old age, full of days, riches and honour' (1 Chronicles 29:28); Joseph of Arimathaea is described as 'a rich man' (Matthew 27:57). There is nothing against wealth as such, it is part of God's gift to man.

(2) There is not a word here against business, against trading, against making profit, against a good commercial instinct, against industry, effort, ingenuity and skill. In fact the Bible says 'Go to the ant, O sluggard, consider her ways, and be wise' (Proverbs 6:6 RSV). We are told

'Never lag in zeal and in earnest endeavour' (Romans 12:11, The Amplified Bible). What the Bible condemns is not busyness but laziness!

(3) This whole passage teaches us the madness – and the menace – of materialism. As the Psalmist puts it, 'If riches increase, set not your heart upon them' (Psalm 62:10). When riches do increase, there is a tendency, a danger and a temptation to set our heart upon them. That is why the Bible gives us this clear word of warning in the first place. Paul underlines the same truth when he writes 'Those who desire to be rich fall into temptation, into a snare, and into many senseless and hurtful desires that plunge men into ruin and destruction' (1 Timothy 6:9 RSV). There is a deadly danger in 'things'. Beware of the menace and the madness of materialism!

(4) This passage teaches the responsibility and reward of stewardship. Let us just remember again that phrase about the rust of their hoarded possessions being a witness or a testimony against these ungodly men. We have all heard of the phrase 'you can't take it with you'. That is obviously true, but this passage teaches an even more challenging truth – that it will be waiting for us when we get there! James says that the rust on the hoarded possessions of these men would be there on the day of judgment, giving witness against them.

I wonder if you have ever studied a most unusual verse in Luke 16. To help grasp its meaning more quickly, let me give it to you from The Amplified Bible – 'And I (Jesus) tell you, make friends for yourselves by means of unrighteous mammon (that is, deceitful riches, money, possessions), so that when it fails, they (those you have favoured) may receive and welcome you into the everlasting habitations (dwellings)' (Luke 16:9). How are we to use our material possessions? We are clearly not to hoard them up. We are not to treasure these things up for ourselves, that is wrong. We are not to squander them on pleasure, that is equally wrong. We are stewards of these things and Jesus said that we should use them. We should use them to make friends, so that 'when it fails' (perhaps an equally valid translation would be, 'when *they* fail', or 'when *they* die') – either that or when your money fails, in other words when you die – they (the people you have helped) will welcome you into heaven. To paraphrase that paraphrase – we are to use our means in the spreading of the gospel throughout the world, so that at the end of life there will be those in heaven who will welcome you there because you gave of your perishable, material possessions here upon earth. That seems to me to be what Jesus is saying here. I can think of nothing more wonderful, nothing that twists the devil's tail more infuriatingly, than to think that these material possessions which, if we let them, will simply go to rust, can actually be taken by us and used to the conversion of other people; that that which is perishable can be used by God to bring about an imperishable miracle in the lives of people we will never see until the day we reach heaven. Imagine that lovely moment when someone will come up to you and say 'Welcome to heaven. I have some wonderful news for you. You know that gift you sent regularly to that missionary society? Well, I was converted through a missionary working under its auspices. I came to Christ through the preaching of a missionary who would not have been there unless you and others had supported that society by sending out your perishable possessions! You sent him out to preach the gospel, and here I am sharing with you an inheritance incorruptible, undefiled and that will never fade away.' What a wonderful thought! This surely is the supreme lesson to learn from all this. This is the way to fulfil the command of Jesus when He said that we were to 'lay up for yourselves treasure in heaven' (Matthew 6:20). What a responsibility! – but what a wonderful reward. Let the madness of materialism help to teach us the Sanity of Stewardship!

Chapter 2

LIVE LOOKING UP!

'Be patient therefore, brethren, unto the coming of
the Lord. Behold, the husbandman waiteth for the
precious fruit of the earth, and hath long patience for
it, until he receive the early and latter rain.

Be ye also patient; stablish your hearts: for the
coming of the Lord draweth nigh.

Grudge not one against another, brethren, lest ye
be condemned: behold, the judge standeth before the
door.

Take, my brethren, the prophets, who have spoken
in the name of the Lord, for an example of suffering
affliction, and of patience.

Behold, we count them happy which endure. Ye
have heard of the patience of Job, and have seen the
end of the Lord; that the Lord is very pitiful, and of
tender mercy.

But above all things, my brethren, swear not,
neither by heaven, neither by the earth, neither by
any other oath: but let your yea be yea; and your
nay, nay; lest ye fall into condemnation.'

(James 5:7–12)

In the opening six verses of this chapter, James has been
exposing and challenging the lives of ungodly rich men
who persecuted and defrauded the poor, and who lived
in careless luxury. Now, from verse 7 onwards, he turns
to speak directly to the Christians who were being persecuted in one way or another; he gives them instructions

on how they are to behave under pressure, and he encourages them to look for a day of deliverance. That, in one sentence, is a summary of this section.

Notice how when directly addressing Christians, he immediately reverts to the use of the word 'brethren'. In verse 7 he says 'Be patient therefore, *brethren*'; in verse 9, 'Grudge not one against another, *brethren*'; in verse 10, 'Take, my *brethren*, the prophets . . . '; and in verse 12, 'But above all things, my *brethren*, swear not . . . '. I find that a very lovely and significant touch! It is a word of sympathy and identification. He has been speaking about the rich, and their oppression of godly people. Now, in turning to the Christians suffering under this pressure, he wants to identify with them and to give them a word of sympathy and comfort. This takes us right back to the opening verses of the epistle – 'James, a servant of God and of the Lord Jesus Christ, to the twelve tribes which are scattered abroad, greeting. My brethren, count it all joy when ye fall into divers temptations'. Immediately he speaks of their problems, their persecutions and their pressures, he uses the phrase 'My brethren'. He feels himself involved in all of their circumstances. He feels for them, and wants to stand with them. Here surely is an immediate challenge to our own hearts! Do we identify with the criticism, the suffering, the oppression and the persecution which Christians are bearing in some parts of the world today? Richard Wurmbrand, a Rumanian Pastor, spent fourteen years in a Communist jail, three of them in solitary confinement. Today, he is dedicating himself to the spread of the Gospel in the world of his tormentors. He has an almost visible burden for the thousands of Christians who are being persecuted for the faith in Eastern Europe today, and in seeking to arouse the consciences of Christians in the free West he often asks 'Why, if you are members of the same body, do you not feel the pain when these people suffer?' That is a deeply challenging question, and one whose principle can be extended throughout the world-wide fellowship of the church. If we are part of the same body, surely we should feel the pain when Christians suffer? We should identify with the hurt inflicted by every blow struck at the body of Christ, whether it be by a Communist government, a religious edict, or a critic's tongue.

Moving into the main body of the passage, I want you to notice that James has three words for these oppressed brethren –

1. *A WORD OF EXPECTATION* – ' . . . the coming of the Lord' (v. 7); ' . . . the coming of the Lord draweth nigh' (v. 8); ' . . . behold, the judge standeth before the door' (v. 9).

These phrases form the context in which the whole passage is framed. For the moment, let us notice just one thing about each of the references James makes here to the second coming of the Lord Jesus.

(1) *It was clear* – 'Be patient therefore, brethren, unto the coming of the Lord' (v. 7). This is James's first reference to the Second Coming of Christ and it is interesting to notice how simple, concise, straightforward and uncluttered the reference is. He simply speaks of the 'coming of the Lord'. You could hardly put a greater truth in fewer words, and the inference seems to me to be clear. No long explanation was needed, because the Christians already knew and believed it. It was a familiar doctrine in the New Testament church. There was no need for James to explain what he meant by 'the coming of the Lord'. It has been said that there are 1,835 biblical references to the Second Coming. It is certainly more easily provable that there are about 300 references in the

New Testament, one for every 13 verses from Matthew to Revelation. But whatever the statistics, the fact of Christ's coming was clear to James and it was immediately clear to his hearers. As the joyous hymn puts it –

> Jesus is coming!
> Sing the glad word;
> Coming for those He redeemed
> By His blood;
> Coming to reign as the glorified Lord,
> Jesus is coming again!

There are three Greek words used in the Bible to describe the Second Coming of Christ. The one used here is the word *parousia*, the word used to describe the arrival of an emperor or a king. It speaks of authority and power. It was the word used by Jesus when He spoke of 'the *coming* of the Son of man' (Matthew 24:27). It was the word Paul used when he spoke of 'the *coming* of our Lord Jesus Christ' (1 Thessalonians 3:13). It was the word Peter used when he spoke of 'the power and *coming* of our Lord Jesus Christ' (2 Peter 1:16). It was the word used by John who said we should live in such a way that when Christ appears we should 'not be ashamed before Him at His *coming*' (1 John 2:28). The word could be well translated 'presence'. That is the moment to which John looked forward and to which James looked forward, and to which quite clearly those to whom he was writing also looked forward.

(2) *It was comforting* – 'the coming of the Lord draweth nigh' (v. 8). Remember the context here. James has been speaking of persecution and of pressure against the Christian church. Some of these Christians – perhaps those who suffered most – must have wondered if there would ever be an end to the persecution and oppression.

James's answer was to point out that the return of Jesus was getting closer all the time, and in the light of that glorious truth he adds 'stablish your hearts' (v. 8). Paul uses the truth of the Second Coming in exactly the same way when writing to the Thessalonians. After speaking of the Lord descending from heaven and the Christians being caught up to meet him in the air, and then going to be with him for ever, he adds 'Wherefore comfort one another with these words' (1 Thessalonians 4:18). Here was a comforting word to the Christians, to those under pressure, to those who wondered if there would ever be an end to persecution, oppression, ostracism and suffering. The Second Coming of Christ remains a comforting doctrine today. Whatever problems we have to face, however difficult our circumstances, however severe the pressures upon us, *Jesus is coming!*

(3) *It was challenging* – ' . . . the judge standeth before the door' (v. 9). In the first two references Jesus is called 'the Lord'. The emphasis is on His Kingship, on His Emperorship, on His Sovereignty in the affairs of the whole universe. 'The Lord' is coming. Now, James very significantly uses a different word, and says, '*the judge* standeth before the door'. Why 'the judge'? The answer clearly lies in the context, and here is something we must note very carefully. James is not at this point addressing the ungodly rich and saying, 'Change your ways because the judge is standing before the door'. He is addressing the *Christians*, and he prefaces this third statement that Jesus is coming with the command 'Grudge not one against another, brethren' (v. 9). We shall examine the meaning of that phrase in a moment, but the point to grasp here is that alongside the clarity and comfort of the Second Coming, James now brings the element of challenge. I am sure you have sometimes heard a con-

gregation told something like this: 'One day you will come face to face with Jesus. Will you meet Him as your Saviour, or as your Judge?' The point of saying that is clear, of course. People are being faced with the matter of whether they have made their peace with God. But on thinking the thing through, it is obvious that it is not really a correct scriptural division. Those are not the alternatives. The truth is that we shall *all* meet Him as Judge. The Christian's salvation will not be in question, of course, but the matter of his reward will be. His life will come under review. 'Every man's work shall be made manifest: for the day shall declare it, because it shall be revealed by fire' (1 Corinthians 3:13). We cannot escape the fact that when James speaks of 'the Judge' here he is addressing *Christians* – in the light and context of their behaviour. We saw this in chapter 4, verse 12. 'There is one lawgiver, who is able to save and to destroy: who art thou that judgest another?' It is the same kind of context. James is warning Christians against being censorious about each other. This was something they had to avoid. Paul says that 'we must all appear before the judgment seat of Christ' (2 Corinthians 5:10). Let us carefully understand what this means. We are to be judged according to our works as Christians. Our reward, or lack of reward, will be based on what we have said, what we have thought, what we have done. Our prayer lives will come under review, so will our stewardship of time, talent and money, every part of our behaviour within the church, within the home, and in the wider context of the world at large. Surely that is tremendously challenging!

On his 90th birthday George Bernard Shaw said 'Our conduct is influenced not by our experience, but by our expectations'. That is a fascinating statement, and worth a moment's careful thought. If we knew that certain events were going to happen, how differently we would act and react! This applies in the home, in the matter of church politics, in the matter of Christian service, in fact, in every part of life. If we could be absolutely certain of future events we would prepare for them. And this is exactly what James is saying here! He is telling us of something that is certain to happen and therefore he exhorts us to behave in a certain way. The expectation of Christ's appearing, of the moment when we shall stand before Him, should colour all that we do, all that we say, everything that we think and all that we are. Martin Luther once said 'I preach as though Christ died yesterday, rose from the dead today, and was coming back tomorrow'. How different our lives would be if lived in that spirit! What a wonderful motto for life! Let me live as though Jesus died yesterday, as though the cross itself had not yet been taken down and could still be seen there on Cavalry as a stark reminder of His great sacrifice for me! Let me live as if He had risen from the dead today, as if it was this morning that the women went to the tomb and saw that the stone had been rolled away; as if the grave clothes were still there 'laid by themselves'! Let me live as if He were coming back tomorrow, as if this was my last day, this my last morning, tonight my last night, today's opportunities my last opportunities!

Here, surely, is the challenge of this word of expectation. Now let us turn to James's second word –

2. *A WORD OF EXHORTATION.* There are in fact four words of exhortation in this passage, two negative and two positive. Let us deal with them in that order.

(1) *Two negative words.*

Firstly, 'Grudge not one against another brethren' (v. 9). The Berkeley Version translates the first word 'complain', the Revised Standard Version has 'grumble', and

the Revised Version 'murmur'. It is not difficult to see
why this sort of word is appropriate at this point. Here
were Christians under severe pressure, and not un-
naturally they began to fray at the edges. They began to
complain and to murmur one against the other. And the
first to suffer from their complaining were Christians,
their own fellow believers. What a deep insight into spiritual truths James shows us here! So often, the first people
to suffer when we begin to crack up are our fellow Christians, our fellow believers. 'Divide and conquer' is not
only a well known military tactic, it is a well known
satanic one too. One of the greatest things that Satan can
do to forward his purposes is to cause division among
Christians – complaining, grumbling, murmuring, fight-
ing, bickering and criticising the one against the other.
Paul was able to say of the devil 'we are not ignorant of
his devices' (2 Corinthians 2:11) and we must certainly
learn this one. The devil has achieved a great victory when
he gets Christians angry and complaining and murmuring
against each other. James has already warned us against
that kind of behaviour in chapter 4, verse 11, where he
says 'Speak not evil one of another, brethren'. There too,
incidentally, he spoke in the context of the judgment to
come – 'He that speaketh evil of his brother, and judgeth
his brother, speaketh evil of the law, and judgeth the law:
but if thou judge the law, thou art not a doer of the law,
but a judge. There is one lawgiver, who is able to save
and to destroy: who art thou that judgest another'.

When reminding the Corinthians of the fate of the
Israelites in the wilderness, Paul says 'Neither murmur
ye, as some of them also murmured, and were destroyed
of the destroyer' (1 Corinthians 10:10). It is always a
tragedy when a Christian 'blows his top', as we say today,
and it is a doubly serious tragedy when he does so within

the fellowship of the church. We can be so terribly un-forgiving on the one hand and so terribly demanding on the other with those who are nearest and dearest to us, those in our own family and those in our own fellowship. Why? – Because the devil loves to wreck a relationship that is likely to bring glory to God. That is something we need to remember very carefully. I remember the first visit that I made to Eastern Europe, some years ago now. I went by car with two other evangelists. It is not for me to suggest their opinions about their companion on the journey! – but they were delightful Christians, men I still love dearly in the Lord. We met together one evening in a town in the south-east of England, and the next morning drove to Dover to catch the cross-channel ferry. We were in something of a hurry, and were already driving when we started to pray for the whole journey – for our safety, for fruitful contacts, effective ministry, and, above all, the glory of God. We covered the whole trip in the spirit of prayer and dependence upon the Lord. But before long the devil was hard at work, doing his utmost to wreck the fellowship within that car. Great blessings were mini-mised, little problems were magnified, and we found our-selves needing to look to the Lord hour by hour for His protection, and for His enabling to overcome the press-ures that were being exerted against us. To His great glory, the whole journey was a happy triumph for the love of God 'shed abroad in our hearts by the Holy Ghost' (Romans 5:5), and, as we can now see, helped to lay the foundation for a wonderful work being carried on in Europe today. But the devil's tactics were clear. Let us learn and re-learn the lesson!

Secondly, 'But above all things, my brethren, swear not, neither by heaven, neither by the earth, neither by any other oath: but let your yea be yea; and your nay, nay;

lest ye fall into condemnation' (v. 12).

This is the second negative exhortation, and it is linked by a similar warning about judgment. This is a long and difficult verse and it will probably be best if we concentrate on the central thing that James is saying here. The background to it is that oaths formed a very important part of Jewish religious and civil life. The writer to the Hebrews, for instance, said that when God made His great central promise to His people, He 'confirmed it by an oath' (Hebrews 6:17). In making that promise to Abraham, 'because He could swear by no greater, He sware by Himself' (Hebrews 6:13). The Apostle Paul also swore by an oath – 'Moreover I call God for a record upon my soul, that to spare you I came not as yet unto Corinth' (2 Corinthians 1:23). There are many other references in the Bible to godly people swearing by an oath, especially in the Old Testament. Then why does James command 'But above all things, my brethren, swear not'?

To discover the answer, we need to probe the background a little further. To put it as simply as possible, oath-making had fallen into disrepute, in two ways. In the first place, some people used them so frequently their oaths lost all significance. Then there were others who divided oaths into two categories, those that were binding and those that were non-binding. It was a binding oath when the name of God was brought into it, but a non-binding oath if a man swore by any other name. A man could swear by heaven, or by earth, or by Jerusalem or even by the hair on his head and because the name of God was not mentioned that was a non-binding oath! In that kind of situation there was obviously a need for the Christian's attitude to be clarified. The whole thing which had always been serious and sometimes sacred, had become a farce and a disgrace. Perhaps this was especially so in times of crisis and pressure, when tempers wore thin. This is the context in which James brings in his word of warning and direction that Christians should not swear by anything, neither by heaven or by the earth, or by anything else.

One ought to add here that in giving this direction, James is not forbidding the taking of an oath in a court of law. Of course there should be no need to take an oath in a court of law. A man should be able to stand in the witness box and have every word of his evidence believed at its face value. But we live in an imperfect world, and the legal structure of oathtaking, with its sanctions against perjury, have become necessary in some measure to guard the accuracy of what is said. It is a concession to the imperfect world in which we live. Oaths have become necessary because of man's inherent dishonesty. But the real lesson here is that in our everyday dealings, and especially in our dealings with Christians, we should be so honest, so straightforward and unambiguous, that no oath or underlining of any kind should ever be necessary. The Amplified Bible puts part of this verse like this – 'let your yes be a simple yes and your no be a simple no'. That is the way we should deal with each other. There should be no need to underline our words, or swear by anything, or to say 'cross my heart' or 'Boy Scouts honour', or anything else. Our yes ought to be yes, and our no ought to be no, beyond any kind of contradiction or compromise or ambiguity. We ought never to need to emphasise that we are telling the truth, because we should never do anything else!

Incidentally, the one other point to notice is that here, as in the other negative exhortation in verse 9, James is warning against the misuse of the tongue. In this particular case he includes a warning against the terrible possibility of taking the Lord's name in vain by taking it lightly, taking it either as an oath or using it casually. In the Tyndale New Testament Commentary, Professor R. V. G. Tasker says at this point 'There are few spheres of conduct in which the young Christian today needs to take the injunctions of the Epistle of James more to heart than in this matter of frivolous and indiscriminate oaths and the thoughtless mention of the Divine Name in general conversation'.

We now move from the two negative words of exhortation, to the

(2) *Two positive words.*

Firstly – 'Be patient therefore, brethren' (v. 7); which is repeated a moment later in the phrase 'Be ye also patient (v. 8). The words 'patient' and 'patience' are used five times in this short passage. They actually translate two different Greek words, one of which is used four times, and the other once. The 'odd man out', incidentally, is in verse 11, yet the meanings tend to blend so closely that we can take its general sense as one. To be patient means so much more than the word which we use in our normal English conversation today. It means to face even the most adverse circumstances with courage and calm. It also means to restrain one's anger and resentment. Taken together the meanings embrace patience with both people and circumstances – and the latter is sometimes easier than the former! It is easier to be patient with circumstances than it is to be patient with people. The Bible says we are to be patient with both! Patience is specifically included in 'the fruit of the Spirit' in Galatians 5:22 (where it is translated 'longsuffering' in the Authorised Version). When Paul speaks of the authenticating marks of a true minister of the gospel, the very first one that he mentions is 'much patience' (2 Corinthians 6:4).

Is your life marked by that? – by patient endurance of affliction, difficulty and pressure, and by a constant restraining of anger and resentment in those circumstances?

Secondly, 'stablish your hearts' (v. 8), or, as The Berkeley Version puts it, 'fortify your hearts'. The word 'stablish' is the same Greek word that is used to translate the two words 'stedfastly set' in Luke's Gospel where we read of Jesus that He 'stedfastly set His face to go to Jerusalem' (Luke 9:51). We could translate that 'He stablished His face to go to Jerusalem'. What a vivid illustration! Jesus knew what was going to happen in Jerusalem. He knew that the pressures were mounting and that His enemies were growing in number and ferocity. He knew that ahead lay desertion, trials, blood, sweat, tears, torture and agonising death. *But that was not all.* Ahead too lay the resurrection, the ascension and eternal glory on the right hand of God! So He stablished His heart; he steadfastly set His face! Notice too that that is exactly the spirit in which the writer to the Hebrews says we are to live the Christian life. 'Wherefore seeing we also are compassed about with so great a cloud of witnesses, let us lay aside every weight, and the sin which doth so easily beset us, and let us run *with patience* the race that is set before us, looking unto Jesus the Author and Finisher of our faith; who for the joy that was set before him endured the cross, despising the shame, and is set down at the right hand of the throne of God' (Hebrews 12:1–2). The Bible does not speak of patience in terms of waiting for something to happen, but rather of stedfast endurance while things *are* happening, and of pressing on regardless of what *will* happen.

Patience is not rooted in fatalism that says everything is out of control. It is rooted in faith that says everything is in His control!

So far in encouraging his readers to 'live looking up' James has given them a word of expectation and a word of exhortation. Now, he gives

3. *A WORD OF EXAMPLE.*

To underline what he is saying, James gives three illustrations –

(1) *The farmer* – 'Behold, the husbandman waiteth for the precious fruit of the earth, and hath long patience for it, until he receive the early and latter rain' (v. 7). Here is a simple illustration of the principle James has been hammering home. The early rain came in late autumn and would germinate the seed. The latter rain came in the spring and would lead to the swelling of the grain toward harvest. Knowing that both were going to come in God's good time, the farmer obediently sowed, carefully cultivated and waited patiently for God to fulfil His promise. That is the point that James is making here, and it hardly needs any application. The farmer knew the promises of God and therefore he worked honestly and waited for God to fulfil His word.

(2) *The prophets* – 'Take, my brethren, the prophets, who have spoken in the name of the Lord, for an example of suffering affliction, and of patience. Behold we count them happy which endure' (vv. 10–11). The persecution of the prophets was a fact of history, so much so that at his martyrdom Stephen cried to the mob 'Which of the prophets have not your fathers persecuted?' (Acts 7:52). It was a by-word. If you were a prophet, you were persecuted. Hebrews 11 gives us a blood-chilling list of the ways in which God's special messengers had been persecuted; by the use of wild animals, by fire and sword, by armies and tortures, by mockings and scourgings, by imprisonment and stoning, by saws and by banishment. Even those chosen by God for positions of special honour

and service had not been immune from suffering and
pressure and persecution – in fact, quite the reverse. They
had been singled out for the worst of the world's rage and
madness. Yet, says James, 'we count them happy which
endure'. That word 'endure', by the way, has the same
root as the word 'patience'. These Christians knew that
those suffering saints had steadfastly endured all the
world's rage and madness and had passed triumphantly
through it all to receive the crown of life, the Lord's 'well
done', and rest from their labours. Now if they had
suffered so much, if they had been persecuted so greatly,
if they had endured so courageously, then should we not
be encouraged to bear our smaller burdens with courage
and hope and patience? This is the issue for us today.
Jesus said 'Blessed are you when men revile you and per-
secute you and utter all kinds of evil against you falsely on
my account. Rejoice and be glad, for your reward is great
in heaven, for so men persecuted the prophets who were
before you' (Matthew 5:11–12 RSV).

(3) *Job* – 'Ye have heard of the patience of Job, and
have seen the end of the Lord; that the Lord is very
pitiful, and of tender mercy' (v. 11). Notice that James
says 'ye have heard of the patience of Job'. Job's patience
was proverbial, and it still is today. We still speak of 'the
patience of Job'. It is a remarkable thing that a whole
major book in the Bible was written to underline this one
virtue – steadfast endurance of adverse circumstances in
the settled assurance of the overruling providence of God.
Job was not perfect. He made mistakes. In modern
language, he 'lost his cool' at times, and especially with
those with whom he discussed his problems. Yet through
it all, his faith in God remained steadfast. At the end of
that terrible day when he lost his family and flocks, we
read that he 'arose, and rent his mantle, and shaved his

head, and fell down upon the ground, and worshipped, and said, "Naked came I out of my mother's womb, and naked shall I return again thither: the Lord gave, and the Lord hath taken away; blessed be the name of the Lord" ' (Job 1:20–21). Later, when the pressures were even greater, his trust in God was so profound that he could say 'Though He slay me, yet will I trust Him' (Job 13:15). Do we begin to match that kind of faith and that kind of patience in our much smaller difficulties and in the pressures and problems which we have to face in our everyday lives?

Finally, notice the one particular thing which James so carefully points out. – He says that his readers 'have seen the end of the Lord; that the Lord is very pitiful, and of tender mercy'; or, as the Revised Standard Version puts it, 'you have seen the purpose of the Lord, how the Lord is compassionate and merciful'. The book of Job only begins to make sense when we recognize that through it all God was at work, and that His ultimate purposes were loving and kind. In material things, of course, the 'end of the Lord' was marvellous indeed, for 'the Lord gave Job twice as much as he had before' (Job 42:10). Again we are told that 'the Lord blessed the latter end of Job more than his beginning: for he had fourteen thousand sheep, and six thousand camels, and a thousand yoke of oxen, and a thousand she asses. He had also seven sons and three daughters' (Job 42:12–13). Yet Job was blessed at a level altogether higher than the material. His character was completely vindicated. His spiritual experience and understanding were enriched beyond measure. God dealt with him in such a way that James could say that the Lord truly showed Himself to be compassionate and merciful.

Here is the note on which to end our study of this section. We live in a world of affliction, pressure and persecution. There are problems in our Christian lives beyond our understanding. There are times when we are tempted to despair, and to crack up, and to give in. But let this establish our hearts – the Lord is coming! We are going to be with Him, and at the end of the day we will see that through it all the Lord has been compassionate and merciful. Even now, we can say in faith, 'Surely goodness and mercy shall follow me all the days of my life: and I will dwell in the house of the Lord for ever' (Psalm 23:6).

To live with that conviction is to live looking up!

Chapter 3

A GOD FOR ALL SEASONS

'Is any among you afflicted? let him pray. Is any
merry? let him sing psalms.'

(James 5:13)

The Duke of Wellington once said 'Life is the art of
guessing what is on the other side of the hill'. Even if that
is a pretty thin philosophy for life, at least it does point
out one thing that all of us know to be true, and that is that
life is never the same for very long. It is seldom a long,
flat existence with nothing happening or changing. Life
is full of variety. There are mountain tops and valleys,
there are clouds and sunshine, there is pain and pleasure,
and sometimes they all seem thrown together in a hope-
less confusion. Generations of philosophers, teachers,
thinkers and leaders of men have wrestled with the problem of how to cope with the changeability of life with
all its triumphs and disasters. Whatever the distilled wisdom of the ages might say, only the Christian has the
ultimate, bedrock answer to the problem – because the
Christian has resources that are denied to the rest of
the world. There is provision for the Christian to cope
with every situation in life, no matter how sudden or
severe the change might be, and the practical, down to
earth James summarizes the Christian's right attitude to
life in these simple words – 'Is any among you afflicted?
let him pray. Is any merry? let him sing psalms'. That
covers everything!

There are two obvious parts to this particular study and

in each of them James describes a condition and then gives counsel on how we should react. In following these through, we shall discover that we have a God for all seasons.

1. *IN TIMES OF PRESSURE* – Is any among you afflicted? let him pray.

First of all, notice

(1) *The condition* – 'Is any among you afflicted?' In order to understand what is being said here, we must first establish the meaning of the word 'afflicted'. The Berkeley Version translates it 'suffering trouble'. The Amplified Bible has 'afflicted, ill treated, suffering evil'. The New English Bible says 'in trouble'. In fact, the two Greek words from which the word 'afflicted' is formed mean 'evil' and 'suffer'. The same root words are used in verse 10 when James speaks of the prophets 'suffering affliction'. If we take all of that together, it becomes obvious that although suffering affliction, of which James speaks here, may include physical suffering, it goes very much beyond that, and includes suffering, pressure, pain or problems of many kinds. In other words James is speaking of unspecified difficulty. Before going into details just notice the phrase 'among you', that is, among you Christians. The question is not being asked in the spirit of 'Is there by any chance someone among you who is afflicted? It has a much more definite sense than that. It is a question that is not really a question at all! It is an assumption that the situation exists. Paul gives us an example of this where he says 'If ye then be risen with Christ, seek those things which are above . . . ' (Colossians 3:1). But the question of a Christian being risen with Christ is not a *possibility*, it is a certainty. The real sense of what Paul is saying here is well brought out in the translation by Dr James Moffatt – 'Since then you have been raised with Christ, aim at

what is above'. That is the kind of formula James is using in the verse we are studying. He knew human life much too well to do otherwise. What he is saying in effect is this: 'There are some of you who are suffering and I want you to know that there is an answer to it all'.

It will help us to open up the implications of this word 'afflicted' if we bear in mind a phrase David used in one of the Psalms when he said 'Many are the afflictions of the righteous . . . ' (Psalm 34:19). Now I know that that verse ends on a positive note, but let us just allow that phrase to sink in – 'Many are the afflictions of the righteous'. Can that statement be proved? In what sense is it true? Let us look at some of the afflictions that face God's people in today's world.

Firstly, there are natural afflictions. There is one sense in which this covers all the other afflictions because all afflictions are in the broadest possible terms brought about by the entry of sin into the world, and are shared by all men. There is no difficulty, no problem, no pressure, no afflictions, no pain, no suffering that is not ultimately the result of sin's entry into the world. Paul even dares to say – 'We know that the whole creation has been groaning in travail together until now' (Romans 8:22 RSV). What that means in detail is surely beyond our understanding, but the Bible teaches us that the whole universe is somehow out of joint as the result of sin. Man has to suffer from the disorganization and disease of nature, including the whole world of plant and animal life. Not only is man not what he was meant to be, and not as he was when originally created, but in some cosmic way, neither is the created world as it was when God created it. The whole created universe has become disorganized as the result of sin, and all men, Christians included, suffer from what we have called natural afflictions as a result.

Secondly, there are physical afflictions. This moves the first point into the particular realm of the physical flesh. In his original state, man was without disease or disorder of any kind. Adam was created in the likeness of God, and that does not only mean moral likeness. It most certainly means that physically he was without defect of any kind. But the entrance of sin immediately brought about the onset, for the very first time in man's history, of disease, disorder, decay, deterioration and ultimately, death. Every fibre of man's physical being became prone to disease in that moment and has remained so ever since, so that there is not one atom of our physical makeup that is not now subject to disease. Of course, modern medicine has harnessed scientific discovery in most brilliant ways, not least within our lifetime, with the result that there are some diseases fatal in our parents' time which can now be cured almost without risk. We can praise God for that, for He has given the means to bring that about. But the fact remains that there is not a single family on the face of the earth that has not known physical affliction of some kind or another. Sometimes that affliction has brought the most savage agony or the most terrible lingering torture of pain. As with natural afflictions, Christians are in no way exempt. We are heirs to that part of the 'many afflictions' of which the Psalmist spoke.

Thirdly, there are mental afflictions. It has been estimated that 50% of the hospital beds in Great Britain today are occupied by people who are not there because of any physical affliction that they have. Another estimate says that one in five of the present population of Great Britain will suffer some kind of marked mental disorder by the time they reach the end of their lives. When you widen that circle even further to include all the mental afflictions and pressures that there are, including those that would not take us to the psychiatrist's couch or the doctor's surgery, how few people today totally escape some kind of mental pressure and affliction! The whole Western civilization in which we live today is geared to success and speed, regardless of the cost in human terms. We live in a rat race. We speak of the law of the jungle as if it were something that was put away when man discovered concrete, but in fact the law of the jungle exists today just as much as ever it did. The weakest goes to the wall. Success too often belongs not merely to the hard working, but to the ruthless and the brutal, and the unquestionable result is that mental pressures of stress and anxiety and fear build up to the most terrifying proportions. Yet again, as with the other afflictions the Christian finds himself caught up in that situation. Do you not sometimes feel the effect of that kind of pressure in the world in which we live? Are you under increasing pressure to succeed, to work harder, to move faster, to cover more ground, to meet an increasing demand? That pressure can come not only at work but at home, and in our church fellowships, in fact, wherever our lives take us, and the result, often unnoticed, and at times more serious, is what we can put under the general heading of mental afflictions.

Fourthly, there are spiritual afflictions. I have grouped mental, physical and spiritual afflictions under different headings and yet it is important for us to know that they are not in water-tight compartments. In his book called 'None of these Diseases', Dr S. I. McMillen says 'Medical science recognizes that emotions such as fear, sorrow, envy, resentment and hatred are responsible for the majority of our sicknesses. Estimates range from 60% to nearly 100%'. Here is the mingling of the physical and the spiritual within our frames and our personalities.

But spiritual afflictions can also be looked at from a distinctly separate angle. The Apostle Paul reminds us that as Christians 'we wrestle not against flesh and blood, but against principalities, against powers, against the rulers of the darkness of this world, against spiritual wickedness in high places' (Ephesians 6:12). While the implications of that statement overlap into the natural, the physical, the mental and the spiritual, it is with the spiritual that we usually associate it. In facing the reality of spiritual afflictions in the world, we need to recognize that we are not just opposed by blind circumstances, or by an unthinking fate, or 'bad luck'. Nor are we merely faced by our own fallen nature. We are in fact opposed by a living, intelligent, powerful and implacable enemy, the devil, who like an enraged lion goes about 'seeking whom he may devour' (1 Peter 5:8). Especially when we think of spiritual afflictions, but clearly not excluding the physical and the mental also, we are faced by a knowledgeable enemy who knows when and where and how to attack us. No wonder we have spiritual afflictions! And there is another important truth to bear in mind here, and that is that the Christian will be subject to greater pressure of this kind than the unbeliever. As the devil's enemy, he above all will have to face spiritual afflictions.

Fifthly, there are special afflictions. I have chosen that phrase quite deliberately, because I believe it to be true. The Christian faces special afflictions. It is interesting to notice how Paul uses the same basic word when he encourages Timothy to take his share of 'the afflictions of the gospel' (2 Timothy 1:8). He is not talking of physical or mental or spiritual afflictions, he is talking about *the afflictions of the gospel*, or, as the Revised Standard Version puts it, 'suffering for the gospel'. Later in the

same Epistle he speaks of 'the gospel for which I am
suffering' (2 Timothy 2:9 RSV), and the word 'suffering'
comes from the same root as 'afflictions'. Further on, he
adds 'As for you, always be steady, endure suffering, do
the work of an evangelist, fulfil your ministry' (2 Timothy
4:5 RSV). Here are 'the afflictions of the gospel', special
afflictions. Afflictions only Christians have to bear. People
sometimes speak rather loosely about 'bearing a cross',
which might be a physical illness, a tyrant of a boss, a
rebellious child, a nagging wife, a chronic toothache or a
thousand and one other things. But as Vance Havner
rightly says, a cross is something that you bear *because
you are a Christian*, that you would not have to bear if
you were not a Christian. It is a special affliction. The
worldling does not bear it. He knows nothing of 'the
afflictions of the gospel'. The man who never bows his
knee in prayer, never opens the scriptures to read them,
never goes to church, never knows these special pressures
and problems. They are special afflictions, reserved for
the people of God.

There is something very significant for us here. Every
Christian is in a battle and, if I may say so very carefully,
the Christian worker is in the front line of that battle. Yet
that is not always understood. One has sometimes heard
unthinking criticism about 'the glamour of evangelism' –
the implication that itinerant evangelists live very comfortably, with more pleasures and fewer problems than
other Christians. That kind of statement is both ignorant
and iniquitous. There is no glamour in the gospel. There
is no glamour in the ministry of a true man of God. The
more I read of scripture and history, the more convinced
I am that the man who is determined to live for God, to
work for God, to sacrifice for God, to set his face against
the world, to give his life, or the main thrust of his life

outside of his normal secular occupation, to the spread of the gospel, is going to suffer special afflictions. One can go further, and say with Paul that 'All who desire to live a godly life in Christ Jesus will be persecuted' (2 Timothy 3:12 RSV). It is interesting to notice that that is exactly the point that James made about the prophets in verse 10, 'Take, my brethren, the prophets, who have spoken in the name of the Lord, for an example of suffering affliction, and of patience'. There is a special affliction that belongs to the Christian and, if we must have a word to define it, there is an extra-special affliction that belongs to what we call the full-time Christian worker. There is always some kind of comfort in compromise, and always a demand in discipleship.

So much for the condition. Now James turns to

(2) *The Counsel* – 'let him pray'. The immediate thing to notice is that while the condition was capable of many different applications and interpretations, the counsel has no deviation or diversity at all – 'let him pray'. This is by no means the first time that James has mentioned the subject of prayer and rather than go over ground already covered in the exposition of earlier verses, let me just concentrate on one aspect which I think will be the most helpful in the context of what James has been saying about the afflictions of God's people. That one aspect is this: *the encouragement the Bible gives us to pray.* Listen to David sharing with us, in Psalm 18, some of the afflictions that he has known in his own life. He speaks of 'the sorrows of death' (v. 4), 'the floods of ungodly men' (v. 4), 'the sorrows of hell' (v. 5), and 'the snares of death' (v. 5). Then comes the turning point when he says 'In my distress I called upon the Lord, and cried unto my God: He heard my voice out of his temple, and my cry came before Him, even into His ears' (v. 6). Almost all of the

rest of that wonderful Psalm is given over to the marvellous outcome of that prayer – 'He drew me out of many waters' (v. 16), 'He delivered me from my strong enemy' (v. 17), 'the Lord was my stay' (v. 18), 'The Lord rewarded me' (v. 20). Then, to bring his own experience into the realm of promise for our encouragement today, he says, 'For thou wilt save the afflicted people' (v. 27). The whole Psalm is a glorious affirmation of the fact that we have in this matter a God for all seasons. Scripture teems with the wonderful truth that God is personally and practically involved in all of the affairs of all of His people, including their afflictions. After Israel had endured over 400 years of slavery, God told Moses 'I have surely seen the affliction of my people which are in Egypt, and have heard their cry by reason of their taskmasters; for I know their sorrows' (Exodus 3:7). He promised the Psalmist 'And call upon me in the day of trouble: I will deliver thee, and thou shalt glorify me' (Psalm 50:15). In the verse that we looked at earlier, and which tells us 'Many are the afflictions of the righteous', the Psalmist goes on to say, 'but the Lord delivereth him out of them all' (Psalm 34:19). The Apostle Peter expresses exactly the same confidence – 'For the eyes of the Lord are over the righteous, and his ears are open unto their prayers' (1 Peter 3:12). What a wonderful encouragement all this is! God is looking, God is listening, and God is longing to deliver His people from all their afflictions; longing to bless them, encourage them, guide them, comfort them, strengthen them, deliver them. No wonder James's counsel to the afflicted Christian is so direct – 'let him pray'!

In 1924 two climbers, Mallory and Irvine, were part of an expedition that set out to conquer Mount Everest. As far as is known, they never reached the summit; and they never returned. After the failure of the expedition, the rest of the party returned home. Addressing a meeting in London, one of them described the ill-fated venture, then turned to a huge photograph of Mount Everest mounted on the wall behind him. 'Everest,' he cried, 'we tried to conquer you once, but you overpowered us. We tried to conquer you a second time, but again you were too much for us. But Everest, I want you to know that we are going to conquer you, for you can't grow any bigger, and *we can*!'

Do you see a spiritual parallel? There is a sense in which our afflictions can never grow any bigger. They can certainly never grow any bigger than God allows. As Paul puts it 'No temptation has overtaken you that is not common to man. God is faithful, and He will not let you be tempted beyond your strength . . . ' (1 Corinthians 10:13 RSV). But we *can* grow 'bigger', by the grace of God. We can grow bigger by the power of prayer. I never tire of reading and laying hold of the truth of that precious word that says 'They that wait upon the Lord shall renew their strength' (Isaiah 40:31). Our afflictions *can* be faced, our mountains *can* be conquered, we can say to the Everests that we face in life, 'You can't grow any bigger, but we can'. And we can do so as we lay hold in prayer upon the power of the living God! Joseph Scriven agrees exactly with the Apostle James when he writes

Have we trials and temptations?
Is there trouble anywhere?
We should never be discouraged:
Take it to the Lord in prayer.
Can we find a friend so faithful,
Who will all our sorrows share?
Jesus knows our every weakness:
Take it to the Lord in prayer.

Yet the Christian can find God to be real not only in times of pressure, but also

2. *IN TIMES OF PLEASURE* – 'Is any merry? let him sing psalms'.

As with the Christian under pressure, we have both condition and counsel here.

(1) *The condition* – 'Is any merry?' The Berkeley Version translates this 'Is anyone feeling cheerful?', The Amplified Bible has 'Is anyone glad at heart?', both the Revised Version and the Revised Standard Version have 'Is any cheerful?', while The Living Bible speaks of 'those who have reason to be thankful'. Basically the word denotes an inner feeling of joy and well being. The root of the word used here is used only four other times in the whole of the New Testament. One is where Paul, grasping the opportunity to give his testimony before the governor Felix says 'I do the more *cheerfully* answer for myself' (Acts 24:10). The other three occur in the story of the shipwreck in Acts 27, when the great typhoon Euroclydon swept down the Mediterranean as Paul and others were on their way to Rome. When panic began to set in Paul cried, 'be of good *cheer*' (v. 22). Some time later, he added 'be of good *cheer*, for I believe God' (v. 25). Much later on in the story, when his confidence somehow seems to have permeated the other passengers, we read 'then were they all of good *cheer*' (v. 36). Now notice this: in the situation before Felix, and in the circumstances of the shipwreck, things were difficult. Paul was under pressure. His very life was in danger. Yet he had a deep inner joy rooted in an unshakable faith in God. Now if he could be cheerful then, how much more should we find opportunity to be cheerful when the sea is calm, when the sky is blue and when we do not have these severe difficulties pressing in upon us? The Christian life is meant to be a cheerful

life. It is the devil's lie that the Christian life is meant to
be morbid, and dull all the time. The Christian life is not
funny – but it should be wonderfully happy! The Bible
says that God 'richly furnishes us with everything to enjoy' (1 Timothy 6:17 RSV), and that 'the kingdom of
God is . . . righteousness, and peace, and *joy* in the Holy
Ghost' (Romans 14:17). Life does have its problems and
pressures, and the Bible never hides the fact. But it is
equally insistent that God pours out upon us, upon every
one of us, every day, untold blessings. I love the word of
the Psalmist when he says 'Blessed be the Lord, who daily
loadeth us with benefits, even the God of our salvation'
(Psalm 68:19). There is something radically wrong if a
Christian is never genuinely glad at heart.

The story is told of a very poor lady – yet one of
those James would describe as being 'rich in faith' – who
was always speaking happily and cheerfully and with
wonderful confidence of going to heaven when she died.
A sceptic was speaking to her one day and said, 'But
suppose you never get there?' The lady replied, 'But I am
bound to. God has promised it, and I am resting on His
word.' The sceptic persisted, 'But what if you were to
reach the very gates of heaven and at the very last moment
you were refused entry?' The lady thought for a moment
and then said, 'Well in that case I would walk around the
walls of heaven all day shouting what a wonderful time I
had had on the way!' There was a genuine sense of joy
about her day to day Christian experience. Laughter and
a happy heart are not out of place in God's word.

So much for the condition. Now let us turn to

(2) *The counsel* – 'let him sing psalms'. The Revised
Version and the Revised Standard Version translate this
'let him sing praise', while The Amplified Bible has
'let him sing praise to God'. The Greek root from which

this phrase comes originally meant, 'to twang, or twitch a stringed instrument with the hands'. The word then went on to refer to sacred singing and music making generally. However, to cut across the technicalities, James's counsel is perfectly clear; if you have an honest reason to be genuinely happy, then praise the Lord! All through the Bible that same counsel is given by example or by directive. David says, 'Give thanks unto the Lord, call upon His name, make known His deeds among the people. Sing unto Him, sing psalms unto Him, talk ye of all His wondrous works. Glory ye in His holy name: let the heart of them rejoice that seek the Lord' (1 Chronicles 16:8–10). The words of the 'Venite' begin 'O come, let us sing unto the Lord: let us make a joyful noise to the rock of our salvation. Let us come before His presence with thanksgiving, and make a joyful noise unto Him with psalms' (Psalm 95:1–2). The early church was a singing church. After the ascension, the disciples 'returned to Jerusalem with great joy: and were continually in the temple, praising and blessing God' (Luke 24:52). After Pentecost we find the early church 'Praising God, and having favour with all the people' (Acts 2:47). The Apostle Paul exhorts Christians to be 'teaching and admonishing one another in psalms and hymns and spiritual songs, singing with grace in your hearts to the Lord' (Colossians 3:16). One of the indications of Spirit-filled men is that they will be 'speaking to yourselves in psalms and hymns and spiritual songs, singing and making melody in your heart to the Lord' (Ephesians 5:19).

In the world in which we live today, technical, austere, brittle and scientific, so much emphasis on singing and praising may seem to some to be utterly irrelevant! Why is it that the Bible insists so much that we should sing, and praise, and make a joyful noise unto the Lord? Let me give you three clear biblical reasons.

Firstly, it identifies the Christian. Let me put that negatively to begin with. The Bible teaches that one of the marks of ungodly men was that even when they acknowledged the existence of God 'they glorified him not' (Romans 1:21). That is one of the marks of the ungodly – he does not praise God. That is why I say that singing praise to God identifies the Christian. It is one of the marks of the ungodly that he does not praise God and it is one of the marks of the godly that he does. Thomas Manton says that 'every new mercy calls for a new song', and as God's mercies are 'new every morning' (Lamentations 3:23), every morning should find a song in our hearts! We are to make a joyful noise unto the Lord – even if for some of us a vocalized version would not be a very tuneful one! Never a day should pass without us praising God. As someone once put it 'It is amazing that man is not always praising God, since everything around him invites praise'. Praise to God identifies the Christian!

Secondly, it prevents sin. Not all sin, of course, but one particular sin. Humanly speaking, what are the things that are likely to produce a happy heart? A calm sea, a blue sky, health, success in business, popularity, comfort. In other words, when things are going well, a man is happy in his heart. But alongside of that, there is another great peril. When everything is going well for a man, he tends to forget God. He sets his affection on 'things on the earth' (Colossians 3:1). He begins to get proud and self-centred and arrogant, and to act as if he had done it all himself. The Bible recognizes this so clearly. The warning to the children of Israel had to be repeated again and again – 'Take heed lest you forget the Lord' (Deuteronomy 6:12). Human nature makes us tend to forget the Lord when

everything is going well, but one of the surest antidotes to
pride is to praise the Lord. Arrogance and adoration
cannot live together!

Thirdly, it glorifies God. We are told that plainly in the
Bible – 'Whoso offereth praise glorifieth me' (Psalm
50:23). What a marvellous encouragement to praise the
Lord! Our praise, our worship, our thanksgiving bring
glory to Him. They give unto Him 'the glory due unto
His name' (Psalm 96:8). Praise glorifies God. No attitude
of heart can ever be more appropriate than this, nor could
words and music ever be put to higher use than to glorify
the Lord. Is it any wonder that David cries out 'O magnify
the Lord with me, and let us exalt His name together'
(Psalm 34:3)?

A God for all seasons! In times of pressure, we are to
pray. In times of pleasure, we are to praise. What a little
gem of a verse this is! Practical, yet deeply spiritual.
Down to earth, and yet up to heaven too. When the world
is on top of you, pray. When you are on top of the world,
praise. In the words of Alec Motyer, 'The Christian has
a God for every circumstance. . . . Our whole life, as we
might say, should be so angled towards God that whatever
strikes upon us, whether sorrow or joy, should be de-
flected upwards at once into His presence'. I cannot think
of a better comment that more perfectly represents the
spirit of this verse. 'Is any among you afflicted? let him
pray. Is any merry? let him sing psalms.'

Chapter 4

THIS QUESTION OF HEALING

*'Is any sick among you? let him call for the elders
of the church; and let them pray over him, anointing
him with oil in the name of the Lord: And the prayer
of faith shall save the sick, and the Lord shall raise
him up; and if he have committed sins, they shall be
forgiven him.'*

(James 5:14–15)

We now have before us some of the most controversial
words in the whole of the Epistle of James. For many
centuries, Christians have been radically and sometimes
heatedly divided on their meaning, importance and
relevance, and those divisions have not merely been between major historical groupings (such as the Eastern
Church and the Western Church) but often between
people who would be united on many other scriptural
issues. In his little book 'Faith that Lives', Frank E.
Gaebelein, taking in verse 16, says 'Few passages in
scripture have been more extensively misinterpreted and
misunderstood than these three verses', and that is no
more than a fair assessment of their controversial nature.

I must admit that in my early years of studying the
Epistle I used to pass over this passage with the merest
comment, and would have welcomed any sign of scholar-
ship hinting that the words might not have been in the
original text! Even much later, when preaching through
the Epistle in greater depth, I left these verses out of the
series of expositions altogether, and dealt with them by

holding discussions among the groups to whom I was
ministering. However, that exercise cannot be repeated
when writing a book, and to be consistent the verses must
be dealt with at the same level and in the same way as all
the rest of the Epistle. It may help to use three headings
in our study, one by way of introduction, the second to
point out some of the many interpretations of the verse,
and the third to outline the basic principles that seem to
me to emerge from the text. Firstly, then, we have

1. *THE PARADOXES THAT ARE SO CONFUSING.*
Before we even turn to anything approaching an exposition of the text, it must be obvious that the verses raise
at least two paradoxes.

The first is that while the directions seem so clear, the
church as a whole tends to ignore them. There can surely
be no doubt about the first part of that statement. James
posits a situation in which a member of the church is
taken ill. The degree of the illness is irrelevant at this
point: what we cannot escape is that in this situation
James lays down certain action that must be taken, both
by the sick man and by the 'elders of the church', in-
volving calling, praying and anointing with oil. The instructions are concise, yet apparently perfectly clear. They
are as specific and direct as, for instance, those which
Paul 'received of the Lord' (1 Corinthians 11:23) concerning the taking of bread and wine in order to 'shew the
Lord's death till He come' (1 Corinthians 11:26). But
how many churches today give them serious weight, and
seek to carry them out? Does it form an uncomplicated
part of the general teaching of the church at large today?
The answer must surely be in the negative. It has been
suggested that with today's huge strides in medicine and
surgery, and the social provisions of the Welfare State, the
need for this ministry by the elders has been greatly re-

duced, and one can understand the reasoning behind the
suggestion, but it does not explain the widespread historical retreat from James's simple words. After all, there
has never been an age in which sickness has not wrought
the most terrible ravages, and even today, lingering and
agonizing diseases still hold sway over multitudes of
people. Without any further attempt to discuss the matter
at this stage, surely this must be seen as a paradox: the
Bible apparently offering a solution to one of man's
greatest problems, and the church largely ignoring it!

The second paradox is not a matter of its use or non-
use, but of the effect produced. Again, James is so uncomplicated – 'the prayer of faith *shall* save the sick, and
the Lord *shall* raise him up'. But is that the universal
testimony of all those who have seemingly obeyed the
instructions? Again, there can be only one honest answer
– no! Sometimes, there has been instantaneous and aston-
ishing healing; sometimes, the cure has been so gradual
and prolonged as to be scarcely identifiable with the
scriptural instructions; at other times, the patient has continued to deteriorate and eventually died of his illness.
Now that, surely, is a paradox. It seems to say 'The Bible
is true, but when we obey it, it does not always work' –
and that statement poses a host of practical and theological problems. Again, let us not attempt any discussion
of the matter at this stage. Let us just acknowledge that
this is the second paradox that faces anyone coming to
these verses with an open mind.

From this introduction, let us now turn to
2. *THE PROPOSITIONS THAT ARE SO CONFLICT-
ING.* In his major Commentary on the Epistle of James,
Thomas Manton writes 'This scripture hath occasioned
much controversy. Though in this exercise I would mainly
pursue what is practical, yet when a matter lieth obvious

and fair, like the angel in the way of Balaam, it cannot be avoided without some dispute and discussion'. His words may seem quaint, but we take his point! Down the years, these two verses have been interpreted in a multitude of ways, and used to support many different quasi-medical practices in the Christian church. While some of the lines followed have been sane and spiritual, some have been patently absurd, while others have stretched all the rules of honest exegesis to breaking-point and beyond. Let us look at some of the propositions that have been made. In doing so, we will still not come to the actual words of the text in order, but we can easily bear them in mind as we go along, will refer to them often, and will look at them in a more positive context later. Here, then, are some of the propositions made about these verses –

(1) *They find expression today in Extreme Unction.* This would certainly be claimed by some, but on what basis can this possibly be maintained? Extreme Unction is one of seven sacraments held as valid by the Roman Catholic Church. The priest anoints with oil a person who is *in extremis*, that is, dying, and prays for the remission of his sins. In its present form, the sacrament was not introduced until the 12th Century, but even if its origins can be traced much further back than that, it certainly has no scriptural basis. The merest glance should prove that there is certainly no connection with these verses in the Epistle of James. Extreme Unction is only given where the suffered is expected to die, whereas James is clearly speaking of someone who is expected to recover. There could hardly be a greater discrepancy! In spite of the footnote to these verses in the Douai Version of the Bible, which says that they provide 'a plain warrant for the Sacrament of Extreme Unction', the case fails at the first test.

(2) *They are the basis for 'divine healing' ministries.*
Some churches that emphasize the question of healing
give a large place to specific people with 'a gift of healing'. This sometimes forms a major part of an itinerant
ministry which includes 'Divine Healing Crusades' and
the like. With no space to comment on these in detail, we
can surely say that these words of James do not form a
basis for them. In the first place, there is no suggestion
by James that anybody in the situation had 'a gift of
healing'. The sick man was to call for 'the elders of the
church', who are seen in the New Testament to be men
called and equipped by the Holy spirit to serve the church
in various capacities. Sometimes called 'bishops', they
were 'overseers, to feed the church of God' (Acts 20:28).
They were to be so qualified that they were 'able by sound
doctrine both to exhort and to convince the gainsayers'
(Titus 1:9). Paul singled out some as those 'who labour
in the word and doctrine' (1 Timothy 5:17). In other
words, they were ordinary people, laymen called by God
to exercise the ministry of caring for the believers by their
oversight of local congregations. In not a single case are
we told of an elder having 'a gift of healing' or of being a
miracle-worker.

Secondly, it is quite plain from the text that James has
in mind a normal 'domestic' church situation, and not a
special event when a 'healer' arrives in town and gets to
work. As Frank Gaebelein puts it 'Whatever else it was,
the scene James described was intimate and personal, not
a public display'. These verses, then, have no direct relationship to 'divine healing' ministries.

(3) *They were only intended for the Apostolic age, and
are no longer relevant.* While this view would be held
with variations here and there, its general dogmatic line
has many weighty supporters. In the 17th Century, John

Trapp said that anointing with oil, 'an extraordinary sign of an extraordinary cure' was only used 'as an outward symbol and sign till miracles ceased'. John Howe, one-time chaplain to Oliver Cromwell, limited the use of James's words to the age when it was 'necessary that frequent miracles should be wrought for the confirmation of Christianity'. The great Matthew Henry wrote tersely 'When miracles ceased, this institution ceased also'. Matthew Poole said that the outward rite was only relevant while the gift of miracles lasted, 'but the gift ceasing, it is vainly used'. John Calvin's judgment was that 'As the reality of the sign continued only for a time in the church, the symbol must have been only for a time'.

Those are impressive statements, yet to endorse their view without qualification raises many questions. Can we agree flatly that miracles have ceased? Are there no places in the world today where 'signs' would be out of place for 'the confirmation of Christianity'? Can we say 'it is vainly used' and that there are no instances of it being used effectively? Can we overthrow the judgment and testimony of other godly men who would take the opposite view?

(4) *This is the only divine prescription for healing, and every Christian should ask for healing in this way.* This is an extreme view, but we should look at it for a moment. The basic objection to the proposition is that it limits God to working in supernatural ways, without recourse to means of any kind. But surely that is nonsense. In the Foreword to his book 'Miraculous Healing', Dr Henry W. Frost explains his choice of the title by saying that 'healing of any kind is necessarily divine. A physician does not heal, nor medicine, nor a scientific diet, nor an improved environment, nor anything else that may be named. All creation or re-creation is from God; and hence, in every

instance of healing He is the One who heals, whether He acts directly through unknown laws or indirectly through known laws'.* The complex healing mechanism of the human body, which is activated by any illness or injury, is a gift from God. Commonsense, which tells an over-wrought man to rest, is a gift from God. Fresh air and sunshine are gifts from God. Vitamins and protein are gifts from God. Medicine is a gift from God. The surgeon's skill is a gift from God. All of these are means God uses to restore health, and we actually limit God when we confine Him to the miraculous.

The second objection to the proposition is that it runs counter to the words of Jesus. Answering those who queried His association with notorious sinners, Jesus said 'Those who are well have no need of a physician, but those who are sick' (Matthew 9:12 RSV). In other words, Jesus used as an illustration of His spiritual ministry the physical fact that sick people need a doctor.

There is the further objection that the proposition conflicts with the experience of the Apostles. In one of his final letters, Paul refers to 'Luke, the beloved physician' (Colossians 4:14), with the clear inference that as a man of God he was honourably able to continue his medical practice. Again, sympathizing with his chronic illness, Paul advised Timothy 'No longer drink only water, but use a little wine for the sake of your stomach and your frequent ailments' (1 Timothy 5:23 RSV). We can surely ask why the elders were not called, if their ministry was the only God-honouring means of restoration.

* I came across this book while preparing this chapter, and found it a great help in trying to focus the meaning of James's words. While not necessarily agreeing with all of its conclusions, I would commend it to any interested in reading more on the subject. "Miraculous Healing" by Henry W. Frost is published by Evangelical Press.

(5) *No Christian need ever be ill, because there is heal-ing in the atonement.* In other words, it is God's invariable intention that His people should always enjoy perfect health, and they may therefore claim it as a right. Theo-logically, this argument rests mainly on Matthew's note that the healing ministry of Jesus was carried out 'to fulfil what was spoken by the prophet Isaiah, "He took our infirmities and bore our diseases" ' (Matthew 8:17 RSV). The quotation is from Isaiah 53:4, where alter-native readings of 'griefs' and 'sorrows' would allow the use of the words 'sickness' and 'griefs'.

Now while it is undoubtedly true that Jesus took upon Himself the Divine judgment on His people's sins, includ-ing the penalty of physical death, it is clearly *not* true that Christians have immediate and complete possession here and now of all the benefits of His death. Ultimately, the Christian will be free from temptation – but for the moment he must still face it. Ultimately, there will be for the Christian no more tears, sorrow, crying or pain – but while he lives on this present earth, these remain facts of life. One day, the Lord will give the Christian a body 'like unto His glorious body' (Philippians 3:21) – but for the moment he must live within his natural, physical limit-ations. Although death for the Christian has lost its sting, being swallowed up in the victory of Christ's resurrection, it is still something he must experience here on earth. It has not been removed from him by the atonement. The same is clearly true about bodily sickness. Paul says that while we already have 'the firstfruits of the Spirit', we are still 'waiting for . . . the redemption of our body' (Romans 8:23).

Put very simply, a dogmatic proposition about 'healing in the atonement' is found to prove too much, and to raise more questions than it answers. Why, for instance, did

Paul have to admit to Timothy 'Trophimus I left ill at Miletus' (2 Timothy 4:20 RSV), instead of persuading the sufferer to claim healing as of right? Why did he allow his beloved fellow-worker Epaphroditus to become 'ill, near to death' (Philippians 2:27 RSV) instead of pointing him to the one sure remedy? Yet it is Paul himself who provides the clinching answer to this argument when he tells us of this 'thorn in the flesh' (2 Corinthians 12:7). Various suggestions have been made as to its nature, the most common being that it was some kind of chronic eye disease. The vital thing to notice is that although he prayed three times for the Lord to heal him, the Lord did not grant his request, telling him instead 'My grace is sufficient for thee: for my strength is made perfect in weakness' (2 Corinthians 12:9). This is obviously a key verse, for it shows that God, in His infinite wisdom, sometimes allows His children to suffer. While He undoubtedly *can* preserve or restore His people from sickness, it is not always His *will* to do so.

The propositions at which we have looked briefly are only some of many, but to look at any more might only add to the sense that these two apparently straightforward verses by James have been little more than a theological and ecclesiastical battleground. Instead, let us try to gather together a positive line of interpretation that seeks to do justice both to history and to the actual text before us. In doing so, perhaps I should say that I shall not quote any 'case histories', as I believe that individual cases make bad law, and can be made to prove almost anything. Many non-Christian religions could produce startling 'evidence' of healing; the devil is capable of 'signs and lying wonders' (2 Thessalonians 2:9); and Jesus prophesied that there would be 'false Christs, and false prophets' who would 'shew great signs and wonders'

(Matthew 24:24). Let us turn instead to the testimony of scripture, and notice from James's words

3. *THE PRINCIPLES THAT ARE SO CLEAR.* In view of all the controversy over the verses, it may seem bold to suggest that they contain any clear principles at all. But I believe that they do, and if we turn now to the text in the light of what we have already studied, perhaps we shall find certain issues falling into place.

(1) *The complaint* – 'Is any sick among you?' The Greek word translated 'sick' has a great variety of meanings, including 'without strength', and 'not functioning properly', but in every case it describes a relatively serious condition. We can therefore be sure that James is not speaking here of a minor discomfort such as a slight headache, or of a person feeling a little below par. This is perhaps confirmed by the fact that the patient has to call for help, the inference being that he is not well enough to go and receive it.

(2) *The call* – 'let him call for the elders of the church'. As we have already seen, these 'elders' were ordinary laymen, ordained by God and recognized by the local church as being in positions of spiritual and practical leadership. The important thing to notice here is that the human initiative comes from the patient. As John Bird puts it 'There is no warrant in Scripture for people running around with bottles of oil healing anyone and everyone. The responsibility rests first with the sick person'. For reasons we shall see later, this is a very serious responsibility.

(3) *The command* – 'and let them pray over him, anointing him with oil in the name of the Lord'. I am sure that, quite apart from the miraculous element, there is a warm, pastoral word here. As Professor R. V. G. Tasker comments, 'While it is true that they could inter-

cede for the sick man without being present at his bedside, nevertheless, by coming to the actual scene of the suffering and by praying within sight and hearing of the sufferer himself, not only is their prayer likely to be more heartfelt and fervid, but the stricken man may well become more conscious of the effective power of prayer . . . ' There is surely an incidental word here for all those in positions of leadership and responsibility within the church. Let them remember that their duties are not primarily institutional, but personal. Their first concern should be for people, not things, and they should continually ask the Lord for that sensitive spirit that enables them with sincerity and understanding to 'Rejoice with them that do rejoice, and weep with them that weep' (Romans 12:15). Happy the church that is served by leaders with that kind of loving, selfless concern!

The directions to the elders continue with the phrase 'anointing him with oil in the name of the Lord'. The use of oil for medicinal purposes was apparently common in biblical times. Isaiah speaks of bruises, sores and wounds that have not been 'softened with oil' (Isaiah 1:6 RSV), and in the story of the Good Samaritan, part of the emergency first-aid given to the wounded man included 'pouring in oil and wine' (Luke 10:34). On the other hand, when Jesus sent the twelve apostles out into Galilee for an intensive ministry of preaching and healing, we read that 'they cast out many devils, and anointed with oil many that were sick, and healed them' (Mark 6:13), and in this case we must surely assume that the oil was not used medicinally, but symbolically. The cures did not stem from the properties of the oil, but from the power of the Lord, working through the apostles. The oil was merely a 'visual aid', perhaps granted by the Lord to help in focusing the faith of the sufferers. The same could be said of the saliva used by Jesus in the healing of the deaf and dumb man (Mark 7:31–37) and the blind man (Mark 8:22–26) and of the clay He used in healing the man blind from birth (John 9:1–41). By the same line of reasoning this would be the significance of the oil here in the situation described by James. Notice also that Jesus did not *always* use these 'visual aids' in performing His miracles, nor did He give any instructions to the disciples to do so in later commissioning them for their world-wide ministry. This makes it additionally clear that the power did not rest in the means, but in the Lord. As Dr A. P. Waterson wisely writes in 'The New Bible Dictionary', 'Great care must be exercised in avoiding the magical in a search for the miraculous'.

(4) *The consequences* – 'And the prayer of faith shall save the sick, and the Lord shall raise him up; and if he have committed sins, they shall be forgiven him'.

I suppose it could be said that it is the dogmatic nature of this phrase that above all has caused the controversy over these verses. If we read 'the prayer of faith *may* save the sick, and the Lord *may* raise him up' there would perhaps be little or no problem! But we do not read that. We are faced with the straightforward assertion that the person concerned *will* be healed. There are those who have sought to 'spiritualize' the words, either by suggesting that even in the absence of physical healing the sufferer will be given a greater measure of grace to bear his illness, and so 'raised up' spiritually, or by saying that as the Christian would one day go to heaven he would be 'raised up' eventually – but neither of these explanations begins to satisfy the demands of James's simple words. He promises that there will be healing from the physical illness!

He also adds a second (but not secondary) consequence, namely that 'if he have committed sins, they shall be forgiven him'. The use of the word 'if' does not mean that the sufferer might possibly be without any sin at all: the Bible makes it clear that no such person exists. James is referring to the possibility of a direct link between the patient's sin and his sickness, the link of cause and effect. This is completely consistent with the Bible's general teaching on the subject. All sickness is the indirect result of man's original sin. It is because of man's sin that 'the whole creation has been groaning and travailing together until now' (Romans 8:22 RSV). As far as human suffering is concerned, Paul says bluntly 'in Adam all die' (1 Corinthians 15:22). All human sorrow, pain, suffering and physical and mental decay stems from Adam's sin. At the same time, let us be quite clear that not all illness is the *direct* result of a person's sin. This *can* be so, of course, both by specific Divine judgment (of which there are many examples in the Bible) and by the natural course of events (venereal disease being a dramatic example), but in the case of the man born blind, Jesus tells us plainly that this is not always true. Thinking the man's blindness to be the result of sin, the disciples asked Jesus whose sin was responsible. Jesus replied 'It was not that this man sinned, or his parents, but that the works of God might be made manifest in him' (John 9:3 RSV). He was not suggesting that these people were sinless, but that their sin did not cause the man's blindness.

The connection between sickness and sin is sometimes shrouded in mystery but there can be no doubting its reality. What James is saying is that if in the case concerned, some sin has caused or contributed to the illness, either by way of Divine chastisement or by what we might call 'natural causes', God will not only heal the man of his sickness, but will also graciously forgive the sin that caused the trouble. In case that begins to sound like the

elders acting in some priestly capacity, with the ability to
secure forgiveness for other people, we should add that
there is an obvious assumption that the sufferer is truly
repentant, and that he is mingling his heartfelt prayers
with theirs.

(5) *The conditions* – ' . . . in the name of the Lord' and
'the prayer of faith'. These two phrases hold the key to
the whole meaning of the verses we have been studying,
and I believe it would not be exaggerating to say that
every historical, ecclesiastical and theological argument
must eventually be settled in the light of their meaning.
Let me illustrate why I believe they are so important.
Two Christians fall ill, and both call for the elders of the
church. They are prayed over, and anointed with oil. One
dies, and the other is healed. Why? Hold their cases
alongside James's words, and see if there can be any
scriptural explanation. In both cases, there are certain
visible factors that can be checked off as identical in each
case. Both are sick, both call for the elders, in both cases
the elders come, in both cases the sufferer is prayed over
and anointed with oil. But two things are missing from
this list, the phrases 'in the name of the Lord' and 'the
prayer of faith'. These are what we might call the *invisible*
conditions, but if we apply the elementary laws of logic to
the verses before us, they become the all-important ones,
the issues that make the difference between success and
failure. Can we really go as far as that? Let us look at the
two phrases in turn.

Firstly, 'in the name of the Lord'. This obviously means
much more than the mechanical repetition of a phrase
such as 'we do this in your Name', which can be empty
and meaningless. In the Bible, a person's name is again
and again consistent with his nature or character. This
explains sudden changes of name, as in the cases of

Abram, whose name God changed to Abraham (Genesis 17:5) on the threshold of his life's work, and Jacob, who became Israel after his dramatic encounter with God at Peniel (Genesis 32:28).

When we come to consider 'the name of the Lord', we see that it is equivalent to the active presence of God in His revealed nature and character. James himself gives us an illustration of this when he refers to prophets 'who have spoken in the name of the Lord' (James 5:10). These men spoke under a Divine mandate, in the same way that Paul was able to say 'we are ambassadors for Christ, God making His appeal through us' (2 Corinthians 5:20 RSV). In exactly the same spirit, Peter refused any personal praise for the healing of the blind beggar, but pointed the people to Jesus, saying that 'His name through faith in His name hath made this man strong' (Acts 3:16). The ministries of all these men were in God's name, according to His will, and on His authority. Only in this way could they be valid. This point is made crystal clear in the Old Testament. When certain people, concerned about the activities of false prophets, asked 'How may we know the word which the Lord has not spoken?', they were told 'When a prophet speaks in the name of the Lord, if the word does not come to pass or come true, that is a word which the Lord has not spoken; the prophet has spoken it presumptuously' (Deuteronomy 18:21–22 RSV).

Now let us apply these principles to the question of healing. James is not saying that whenever a Christian falls ill he must immediately ask the elders to anoint him with oil. The calling of the elders, and their response, are not automatic, press-button procedures for healing. If they were, there would presumably be no need for a Christian to die at all, as he could avert death whenever it

threatened him by calling for the elders! The plain truth
is that the actions James describes will only be effective
when carried out 'in the name of the Lord', in other words
in accordance with His will, on His authority. There must,
therefore, be a conviction of the Holy Spirit that it is right
to call the elders, and as 'God is not the author of confusion' (1 Corinthians 14:33) we may expect that when
there is, the elders will have a similar witness that the
course of action is right. Not only should the anointing
(and, as someone has pointed out, the simultaneous
prayer) be 'in the name of the Lord', but there must be

Secondly, 'the prayer of faith'. This reminds us so much
of James's earlier command to the person seeking spiritual wisdom – 'Let him ask in faith, nothing wavering'
(James 1:6), and, as we shall see in a moment, fits in
exactly with what we have already discovered about acting 'in the name of the Lord'. What, then, is the meaning
of 'the prayer of faith'? Let us turn to the Bible for the
answer, and discover it first by means of a specific definition and then by a general principle. The specific definition is given to us by the Apostle Paul, when he says that
'whatsoever is not of faith is sin' (Romans 14:23), or, to
quote the very helpful elaboration in The Amplified Bible,
'For whatever does not originate and proceed from faith
is sin – that is, whatever is done without a conviction of its
approval by God is sinful'. In other words, the prayer of
faith is prayer offered with the definite conviction that it
has God's approval. Turning from the specific definition
to the general scriptural principle, we need to recognize
that the whole section from verse 13 to verse 18 is concerned with the subject of prayer. James refers to prayers
of intercession and thanksgiving (v. 13), prayer for the
sick (vv. 14–15), prayer for each other (v. 16) and, by
way of example, the prayers of Elijah (vv. 17–18). With

that in mind, we must approach any interpretation of the passage with the understanding that it must be subject to the biblical laws that govern prayer. We cannot interpret one verse about prayer in a way that makes nonsense of the general teaching of scripture on the subject.

Now let us follow this line of thought in the light of the fact that James 'guarantees' the success of 'the prayer of faith'. Are there other verses that open the door just as widely? Is there one general law in the Bible in regard to successful prayer? The answer to both questions is in the affirmative. While particular aspects of the matter are dealt with in other places, there are at least seven occasions when this one controlling truth is stated. Let us look at them together. The first five are statements of Jesus, and the other two come directly from the pen of the Apostle John – 'Again I say unto you, that if two of you shall agree on earth as touching any thing that they shall ask, it shall be done for them of my Father which is in heaven. For where two or three are gathered together *in my name*, there am I in the midst of them' (Matthew 18:19–20). 'And whatsoever ye shall ask *in my name*, that will I do, that the Father may be glorified in the Son' (John 14:13). 'If ye shall ask any thing *in my name*, I will do it' (John 14:14). 'Ye have not chosen me, but I have chosen you, and ordained you, that ye should go and bring forth fruit, and that your fruit should remain: that whatsoever ye shall ask of the Father *in my name*, He may give it you' (John 15:16). 'Whatsoever ye shall ask the Father *in my name*, He will give it you' (John 16:23). 'And whatsoever we ask, we receive of Him, because we keep His commandments, and do those things that are *pleasing in His sight*' (1 John 3:22). 'And this is the confidence that we have in Him, that, if we ask any thing *according to His will*, He heareth us: And if we know that He hear us, whatsoever we ask, we know that we have the petitions that we desired of Him' (1 John 5:14–15).

On that evidence (which merely supports the obvious truth that must follow from the Bible's revelation of the nature of God) it is clear that all the laws of prayer are eventually governed by this one principle – *to be successful, prayer must be according to God's will.* It is difficult to see that any Christian would wish to dispute that. Furthermore, we cannot alter God's will by our goodness, our persistence, nor even by our faith. This, incidentally, is the answer to the cruel assertion made by some people that anybody can be miraculously healed 'as long as they have enough faith'. That is plainly not true. We cannot alter God's will by an effort of faith, nor by 'claiming' something He has not promised or designed to do. As Spiros Zodhiates puts it, 'If God does not will a thing, neither medicine nor prayer will accomplish the results which we want. His results will come to pass, and happy is the man who is satisfied with the fulfilment of God's wishes rather than his own'.

We need to have this clearly in our minds if we are to have a sane grasp of these verses. As Henry Frost makes so clear in his book, Jesus was sovereign as to the people whom He healed (He did not go everywhere and heal everybody); as to the conditions which He imposed upon men as a means of physical healing (He did not, for instance, always insist on their being disciples); in the limitations which He put upon Himself in His acts of healing (He allowed many people to remain ill in spite of having the power to heal them); as to the persons to whom He gave the gift of healing (only 82 people in all); and in making the Holy Spirit sovereign in His miracle administration (the Spirit granting His gifts according to His own will).

From this over-ruling truth it would seem right to infer that 'the prayer of faith' is not something that man can produce at will, by the repetition of certain words or in any other way, but is, rather, a gift from God, something that can only rightly be prayed when the Lord gives assurance that its substance will be answered in accordance with His own sovereign purposes. This is perhaps underlined by the fact that the word James uses for 'prayer' is not the usual New Testament word. The word normally used comes from a compound Greek word which we could literally translate 'prayer towards'. In this case, James does not use the 'towards' part of the word, perhaps to draw our emphasis away from the human action and to place it on the Divine will. Be that as it may, he certainly underlines this point in the illustration about Elijah which he gives a few verses later. As we shall see in our detailed study of verses 17–18, the success of Elijah's prayers, both for drought and rain, depended not upon his own merit or effort, but upon God's determination to bring these things about, a determination He revealed to Elijah before the prophet turned to prayer. In other words, we could say that the prayer of faith is circular in shape. It begins and ends in heaven, in the sovereign will of an all-wise God.

From this, we can go on to say that the primary thing in the whole situation is the glory of God, the working out of His will; and we need to remember that He can accomplish this in any of the circumstances that might follow a Christian's illness. Healing by the body's natural processes can be to the glory of God; healing by medical means can be to the glory of God; healing by supernatural intervention can be to the glory of God; *and so can the death of the sufferer.* Notice how clearly this comes across in Paul's great statement to the Christians at Philippi, when he tells them that his over-arching concern is that 'Christ shall be magnified in my body, whether it be life, or by death' (Philippians 1:20). The important thing is not health or sickness, but the glory of God.

In the light of all that we have seen, what should a Christian do when he is taken ill? Should he always and immediately go through the outward procedure of calling the elders, and being prayed over and anointed, and then assess God's will by the outcome of the process? Surely not! While our faith in the omnipotent power of God will always encourage us with the possibility of praying for healing, the seriousness of the issues involved should prevent us praying recklessly.

The ultimate concern of this passage is not physical at all, but spiritual, and its most important theme is not the health of man, but the glory of God. As we have seen, 'the prayer of faith' is prayer made 'in the name of the Lord', that is according to His will. But how can we know His will? Paul admits quite frankly that 'we do not know how to pray as we ought' (Romans 8:26 RSV), and it would seem that Paul's own prayer for deliverance from his thorn in the flesh is an example of this. Yet the Apostle himself gives us the answer to his question when, in the same verse, he says 'the Spirit helps us in our weakness'. Effective prayer (and notice how perfectly this all holds together) is prayer that is God-initiated, God-energized. It is not meant to be a spiritual fire-engine, brought in to deal with emergencies, but something that is a continual expression of a Spirit-filled life. The Christian is therefore lovingly commanded to 'walk by the Spirit' and not to 'gratify the desires of the flesh' (Galatians 5:16 RSV).

When he does, he will rejoice in being subject to the Lord's will, and thus bringing glory to His name, and, in Alec Motyer's fine words, 'the disposing of the welfare of a child of God cannot be left with greater confidence anywhere else than in the Father's hands, nor can any solution of the plight be more fitting, beneficial and glorious than that which He has in mind'.

Chapter 5

THE POWER OF PRAYER

'Confess your faults one to another, and pray one for another, that ye may be healed. The effectual fervent prayer of a righteous man availeth much.

Elias was a man subject to like passions as we are, and he prayed earnestly that it might not rain: and it rained not on the earth by the space of three years and six months.

And he prayed again, and the heaven gave rain, and the earth brought forth her fruit.'

(James 5:16–18)

There is a tradition that James was nicknamed 'Camel Knees', because his knees had become calloused and hardened through the time he spent in prayer. While I have no means of authenticating the tradition, I do know that anything that would tell us that James was a man of prayer would be borne out by the Epistle that he has written for us. The importance of prayer comes through again and again. In chapter 1, verses 5–6, he says, 'If any of you lack wisdom, let him ask of God, that giveth to all men liberally, and upbraideth not; and it shall be given him. But let him ask in faith, nothing wavering'. At the beginning of chapter 4 he examines the reasons for defective prayer – ' . . . ye have not, because ye ask not. Ye ask, and receive not, because ye ask amiss, that ye may consume it upon your lusts'. Now, the whole of the section from verses 13 to 18 of this particular chapter is given over to prayer in one aspect or another. Certainly prayer is the subject dealt with in verses 16 to 18, and we will be helped to understand it if we see three distinct points.

1. *A VITAL DOCTRINE* – 'The effectual fervent prayer of a righteous man availeth much' (v. 16b).

This phrase not only lies in the centre of the section in terms of the words that James used, but it lies at the very heart of the section in terms of its importance. This is the hub around which the whole of the section revolves. It is the rock on which the whole section is built. It is the doctrinal basis for the practical outworking of everything else. Taking the words in the order in which they occur, notice these three things:

(1) *The intensity of the asking* – 'The effectual fervent prayer'. This is a clumsy sort of phrase in the Authorised Version, partly because the words 'effectual fervent' translate a single Greek word. It is from the root of this word that we get our English word 'energy', and that moves us partly towards unlocking the meaning of the phrase. Negatively (to clear away some of the rubble before we start building), in order for prayer to be effective it does not have to be phrased in religious language. An American lady is said to have visited Israel very late in life and on her return home she started taking a course in Hebrew. When someone asked her why she was taking up this very difficult language so late in life she replied, 'Well, it will not be long before I die, and when I do I would love to greet my Maker in His native tongue'! There is no need to pray in Hebrew, or Greek, or the language of the Authorised Version, nor in any special 'religious' language in order for prayer to be effective. Neither does prayer have to be long-winded in order to be effective. Somebody has pointed out that most of the prayers recorded in the Bible are very brief. Peter's 'Lord

save me' (Matthew 14:30) could not have been briefer –
nor more effective! The publican could only blurt out
'God be merciful to me a sinner' (Luke 18:13), but he was
saved as a result! Even the most magnificent prayer in the
whole Bible, in John 17, only takes a few minutes to read.
Length, then, is not important.

It would also seem clear that the all-important thing in
prayer is not frequency. We are certainly told to 'Pray
without ceasing' (1 Thessalonians 5:17) but that does not
mean that frequency in prayer is of first importance. Jesus
said, 'But when ye pray, use not vain repetitions, as the
heathen do: for they think that they shall be heard for
their much speaking'. The essential thing is clearly not a
mere multiplication of words, or frequency of prayer.
That could be no more than 'vain repetitions'. What *is*
important, according to James here, is *fervency* in prayer.
Jacob wrestled with God (in the form of that strange
visitor) and cried, 'I will not let you go unless you bless
me' (Genesis 32:26 RSV). Paul told the Colossians that
Epaphras was 'always labouring fervently for you in
prayers'. The early disciples 'devoted themselves to
prayer' (Acts 1:14 RSV). Here is the difference between
just saying prayers, or saying prayers very often, or saying prayers in rather rounded and beautiful language and
actually praying – getting through in prayer. It is easy to
say our prayers, but to be fervent in prayer is both difficult and costly – yet it is essential. One old commentator
put it like this – 'If the arrow of prayer is to enter heaven,
we must draw it from a bow full bent'. That hardly needs
any kind of explanation! – and it very accurately reflects
what James is saying, because the word translated
'effectual fervent' could literally be translated 'stretched
out'. It is the kind of phrase you would use of a horse
leaping over a very high obstacle, stretched out to the

fullest limit of its ability, or of an athlete, bursting for the
tape with his last gasp of energy. This is surely a long
way removed from the average Christian's average
prayer! I think that a lot of Christians are sometimes
stretched out in prayer, but only because they are lying on
their beds muttering a few words before they drop off to
sleep! When the Bible wants us to be stretched out in
prayer, that is not what it has in mind! As somebody once
put it – 'No man is likely to do much good in prayer, who
does not begin by looking upon it in the light of a work to
be prepared for and persevered in with all the earnestness
which we bring to bear upon subjects which are, in our
opinion, at once the most interesting and the most necessary'.

But there is something else that needs to be said about
this word and unless we grasp this we will not really sense
what James is getting at here. The phrase translated
'effectual fervent' is almost without exception in the New
Testament used of *God at work*. To understand that is to
get to the real heart of what James is teaching us here. To
give just one example: the Apostle Paul speaks of 'the
word of God, which is at work in you believers' (1 Thessalonians 2:13 RSV). The same phrase is used, teaching
us that God alone can apply His word to our hearts. In
just the same way, only God can enable us to pray fervently, and therefore effectively. To put it another way,
if our prayer is going to be effective, it must be Divinely
energized. When James speaks of 'effectual fervent
prayer' he is speaking of Divine energy at work! Perhaps
one should make an important point here, and that is that
Divine energy at work does not always mean a noise.
When did you last hear a loud sunset? It all happens very
quietly, but what tremendous power is at work! When did
you hear the dawn break? – but what vast energies are at

work! Flowers open silently but what power is at work!
So, for prayer to be effective, it does not have to be noisy,
excitable or spectacular – it has to be Divinely energized.
That is what James is saying here, and in doing so he
agrees exactly with Paul, who wrote 'Likewise the Spirit
helps us in our weakness; for we do not know how to pray
as we ought, but the Spirit Himself intercedes for us with
sighs too deep for words' (Romans 8:26 RSV). The intensity of the asking!

(2) *The integrity of the asker* – 'of a righteous man'.
Here is another bedrock principle of effective prayer. For
a man's prayer to be effective, it must not only be Divinely
energized, but the man himself must be a righteous man.
The Jews seemed to have had a proverb about this, because they told Jesus quite plainly that 'God does not
listen to sinners' (John 9:31 RSV). This matches the Old
Testament statement that 'He hears the prayer of the
righteous' (Proverbs 15:29 RSV). So James speaks of the
prayer of 'a righteous man'. The word 'righteous' is used
in the Bible in two senses. It is used in what we might call
the spiritual sense and the moral sense. Let us take an
example of each. 'There is none righteous, no not one'
(Romans 3:10). There, the word seems to be used in a
spiritual sense. No man can stand before God clothed in
his own righteousness. So, if it is true that the effectual
fervent prayer of a righteous man is the only prayer that
God answers, and none of us is righteous, then none of
us can pray effectively! But that is not the sense in which
James is using the word here. In any event, we could say
that for the Christian, that position has been totally
changed, because 'Christ is the end of the law for
righteousness to everyone that believeth' (Romans 10:4),
or, as Paul says to the Corinthian Christians, the Lord
Jesus Christ is 'made unto us . . . righteousness' (1 Cor-

inthians 1:30). So we do stand righteous before God, because we are clothed in Christ's righteousness alone. But (and here we must follow the argument very closely) does that mean that all our prayers are always effective because we are righteous? We know the answer to that; and the answer is no. Every prayer of every Christian is not answered in the positive way to which James refers here. This makes it crystal clear that he is not using the word in the spiritual sense.

Now for an example of the use of the word in its moral sense. The Apostle John writes 'He who does right is righteous' (1 John 3:7). In other words what a man is positionally, is linked to what a man is experimentally and practically in his daily life. As Robert Law put it, 'Doing is the test of being'. Now it is in this moral sense that James is using the word here, and in doing so he is showing its importance when it comes to effective prayer. It is not enough for a man to say 'I am a Christian', in other words that he is righteous positionally, in terms of justification; a man must also be righteous morally, practically, if his prayer is to be effective. That truth is underlined throughout the Bible. David says 'If I regard iniquity in my heart, the Lord will not hear me' (Psalm 66:18). Isaiah says 'Behold, the Lord's hand is not shortened, that it cannot save; neither His ear heavy, that it cannot hear: but your iniquities have separated between you and your God, and your sins have hid His face from you, that He will not hear' (Isaiah 59:1–2). The Apostle John puts the same truth from the positive angle when he writes 'And whatsoever we ask, we receive of Him, because we keep His commandments, and do those things that are pleasing in His sight' (1 John 3:22).

The Old Testament has a deeply challenging illustration of this truth, in the story of Joshua and his leadership of the people of Israel. After the conquest of Jericho, they came to the comparatively insignificant town of Ai. Based on reconnaissance, Joshua decided that there was no need to commit his whole army to this particular battle. Two or three thousand men would do to deal with this little affair. But his army met with humiliating defeat. In the hour of disaster Joshua did what perhaps we would expect a spiritual leader to do – he called the leaders of the people to prayer. All day long Joshua and the elders lay on their faces and called upon God. And what did God do? He stopped the prayer meeting! Today, it is difficult to start one! – but in this case, God stopped it. 'The Lord said to Joshua, "Arise, why have you thus fallen upon your face? Israel has sinned; . . . therefore the people of Israel cannot stand before their enemies"' (Joshua 7:10–12 RSV). The rest of the story you know. Investigations were made. The culprit, Achan, was discovered, and his sin confessed and judged. When that was done – *and only then* – the people of Israel went on to further victory. Moral righteousness was essential. The integrity of the asker! Now notice

(3) *The immensity of the answer* – 'availeth much', or as the Revised Standard Version puts it 'has great power in its effects'. I have called this particular section 'A Vital Doctrine', because the word 'vital' means 'belonging or contributing to life', and James's teaching on prayer is a living doctrine. It is not merely something for the theologians to discuss. It is living, dynamic, practical, effective. Prayer works! – or, to put it more accurately, God works through prayer. This is the point that James is making. The 'effectual fervent prayer', the Divinely energized prayer of a man who is walking with God is tremendously powerful in its effects. It is one of the means of grace, it is a channel of blessing, it is a way that God uses to bring

about His purposes. As Tennyson wrote in Morte
d'Arthur –

> *More things are wrought by prayer*
> *Than this world dreams of. Wherefore let thy voice*
> *Rise like a fountain for me day and night;*
> *For what are men better than sheep or goats*
> *That nourish a blind life within the brain,*
> *If, knowing God, they lift not hands of prayer,*
> *Both for themselves and those who call them friend;*
> *For so the whole round world is every way*
> *Bound by gold chains about the feet of God.*

God works through prayer! 'The effectual fervent prayer
of a righteous man availeth much'. May God take that
word to our hearts and encourage us to pray and to pray
effectively to His glory!

From this vital doctrine James now turns to

2. *A VIVID DEMONSTRATION* – 'Elias was a man
subject to like passions as we are, and he prayed earnestly
that it might not rain: and it rained not on the earth by the
space of three years and six months. And he prayed again,
and the heaven gave rain, and the earth brought forth her
fruit' (v. 17).

James could have chosen many Old Testament examples of the effective, persistent prayer of righteous men.
He could have given us the example of Moses, who 'fell
down before the Lord forty days and forty nights'
(Deuteronomy 9:25); or Samuel, who 'cried unto the
Lord all night' (1 Samuel 15:11); or Daniel, who 'kneeled
upon his knees three times a day, and prayed, and gave
thanks before his God' (Daniel 6:10). We can be sure that
all of the prophets, and many others, were men of prayer
too, but James chooses Elijah (called Elias in the AV of
this verse). The reason he chose Elijah was possibly

that to the Jews, Elijah represented the prophets in the same way that Moses represented the law. You will remember, for instance, that at the Transfiguration, it was Moses and Elijah who appeared with Jesus on the mountain-top. Be that as it may, two things stand out in this illustration.

(1) *Natural weakness.* Elijah was a man 'subject to like passions as we are'. This is the first thing that James wants to show us. He is not using an extraordinary man, some kind of superman, to make his point. In the original Greek, the order of the words is this: 'Elijah man was he of like infirmities with us'. In other words, the emphasis, in the order of the words, is 'Elijah, *man* was he'. Not superman; just man. He was 'of like passions as we are', or, as the Living Bible paraphrases it, 'completely human as we are'. He was a prophet but he was not perfect. He was prone to all of our failures and weaknesses and sins. He was susceptible to all of our diseases. He was simply a man. We might say that in some senses he was no better than we are. He was in no way exempt by nature from temptation or trial, nor were these things in any particular way held back by God from striking at him. Nowhere in the story of Elijah does that come across more vividly than in the account of what happened after that tremendous victory at Mount Carmel over the prophets of Baal. With no attempt to gloss over the imperfection of one of the greatest Old Testament heroes, the Bible tells us that after that, Elijah, as you will remember, came face to face with the threat of the wicked Jezebel and ran for his life. The man who had defied in the Name of God hundreds of prophets, now ran away from one devil-inspired woman. He ran off into the wilderness, lay down under a juniper tree and wished himself dead, crying 'O Lord, take away my life, for I am not better than my fathers' (1 Kings

19:4). Strange as it may seem, that story of Elijah's depression can be a wonderful encouragement to us. The story of Elijah on the mountain, opposing the prophets of Baal, may make us feel that that is something right outside of our kind of experience. If so, then we fail to grasp the point James is making. His concern is not to show Elijah as an extraordinary man, involved in miracles, but as an ordinary man who knew the humiliation of defeat, and who could put his head between his knees and wish himself dead. And why should that encourage us? Because it is this man who, as Thomas Manton put it, 'seemed to have the key to heaven, to open and shut it at pleasure'! It was this man, sometimes seen at the end of his tether, who was such a mighty instrument in the hands of God.

You get the same truth in the only other verse in the New Testament where the same phrase used by James is used by Paul. It happened when Paul and Barnabas were at Lystra. Paul healed a man who had been crippled from birth, and in a flash he and Barnabas were mobbed. The crowd thought that they were two gods, Jupiter and Mercurius, and were about to offer sacrifices to them when Paul and Barnabas cried, 'Men, why are you doing this? We also are men, of like nature with you' (Acts 14:15 RSV). The danger in reading of outstanding incidents connected with men and women in the Bible is to think that the people involved almost lived in a different world, breathing different air. But they did not! They lived in our world, and they were ordinary people, just as Elijah was an ordinary person, in the sense that he was subject to all of our sins and failures and weaknesses. They were fallen and fallible. The secret of their success lay in the maintenance of their relationship with God. And their God is ours!

From natural weakness, we now turn to notice

(2) *Supernatural power.* This takes in the remainder of verses 17 and 18. The interesting thing to notice in this story is that neither of the prayers at the beginning and the end of the drought is mentioned in the Old Testament story of Elijah told in 1 Kings 17 and 18. What we read is that one day Elijah went to the idolatrous King Ahab and said 'As the Lord God of Israel liveth, before whom I stand, there shall not be dew nor rain these years, but according to my word' (1 Kings 17:1). There is no mention of a prayer, yet the implication seems clear. God revealed His intentions to Elijah. He told him that He was going to stop up the heavens for three and a half years, and in the light of God's revealed will, Elijah was able to pray earnestly and confidently for this very thing. When the drought did eventually come about, then it happened according to God's word, and according to Elijah's prayer.

After the drought began, we have an interval during which there is the story of the dried up brook at Cherith, when Elijah was fed by the ravens, and then the incident at Zarephath where we have the miracles of the cruse of oil and the barrel of meal that never failed, and the raising from the dead of the widow's son. In the third year after that (which would comfortably accommodate the three years and six months to which James refers), the Lord said to Elijah, 'Go, shew thyself unto Ahab; and I will send rain upon the earth' (1 Kings 18:1). Now we are no longer in the realm of conjecture. God *did* reveal to Elijah that the drought was going to end, and I have no doubt that when he heard this Elijah both praised God for it, and *prayed for it to happen.* In other words, Elijah harnessed his prayers to the revealed will of God. We certainly know, from the Old Testament narrative, that when the rains did come Elijah was on the top of Mount Carmel again with his face between his knees, in prayer, stopping every few minutes to ask his servant for a weather report! He was *praying* on the day when the rains returned, and after some time 'the heaven was black with clouds and wind, and there was a great rain' (1 Kings 18:45). This, briefly, is the story of a man and a miracle, or rather, a succession of miracles. And the link between the man and the miracles is this – 'he prayed earnestly'. Literally, those words could be rendered 'he prayed with prayer'. As far as Elijah was concerned, there was nothing else in it but prayer. But it was prayer that was Divinely energized and Spirit led and was therefore able to claim God's promises. This is the one central thing to which James points us in this vivid demonstration.

Now to the third part of our study, in which we find
3. *A VALUABLE DIRECTIVE* – 'confess your faults one to another, and pray one for another, that ye may be healed' (v. 16a).

This is the only directive in the whole of this section of two verses. The middle part is a doctrine – James states a fact concerning prayer. The third part is a demonstration of it – an Old Testament illustration of the truth. Here, we have the directive, the instruction – 'Confess your faults one to another, and pray one for another, that ye may be healed'. I think we can safely say that this phrase is connected not only with those that follow, the doctrine and the demonstration, but also with the previous passage about healing. The Revised Standard Version opens verse 16 'Therefore confess your sins one to another', and several other translations insert the word 'Therefore'. The reason for the connection appears fairly obvious. The healed man is another demonstration of the power made available through prayer. If prayer makes that kind of power available, we ought to pray more often, and more earnestly! Having spoken about the raising of the sick man, through prayer by God, it would be natural for James to go on and speak about some other aspect of prayer. But this particular sentence also introduces another subject, namely the confession of sins, not directly to God, but to other people or, perhaps more accurately, in the presence of other people. Now this, like the matter of healing, is a subject that has given rise to unwise extravagances in all directions, so let us try to get the statement into both biblical and practical perspective.

Firstly, notice the area in which confession should be made – 'Confess your faults *one to another*'. Now it is on this verse in particular that the Roman Catholic church bases its doctrine of auricular confession – confession to a priest – which is obligatory for Roman Catholics at least once every year. Yet it seems to me to be so obvious that that interpretation will not hold water. There is no suggestion here that one man is to be the depository for the confessions of the sins of a multitude of others. It quite clearly says 'Confess your faults *one to another*'. As Martin Luther said, 'A strange Confessor; his name is one-another!' On the other hand, the verse does not mean that every Christian in the world is to go around confessing every one of his sins to every other Christian he ever meets. The result would obviously be carnal chaos, and glimpses of the danger of that sort of thing can be seen from the history of certain groups that have emphasized the confessional element in their personal relationships. Yet the Bible does endorse the doctrine of confession of sins to other Christians. Jesus said 'So if you are offering your gift at the altar, and there remember that your brother has something against you, leave your gift there before the altar and go; first be reconciled to your

brother, and then come and offer your gift' (Matthew
5:23-24 RSV). Here is a clue to one area in which confession should be made – it is to the person who has been
wronged. If I have sinned against a brother in the Lord,
and the Spirit of God reveals that to me, then I should go
and confess that sin to him. That is certainly one area in
which confession should be made.

But there is another, and perhaps even more costly
area, and that is when we feel the need of someone's
counsel in dealing with a particular problem or failure –
when, because of someone else's experience, their knowledge of life, their background, their walk with God, their
knowledge of the scriptures, we feel that we will be helped
if we go and speak to them about some failure, or problem, or sin. This is another area in which confession
should be made.

*Secondly, notice the attitude in which confession should
be made* – 'and pray one for another'. James will not
allow us to stray away from this subject of prayer!
Whether the problem is physical, mental, spiritual, moral
or any other kind, he only knows one sure answer – *pray*!
If a man is sick – *pray*! If you have faults – *pray*! And
'pray one for another'. This is the attitude in which we
should approach one another, or in which we should receive the confessions and confidences of another person.
As someone put it – 'Confession may be made to anyone
who can pray'. We are not to confess our sins in a spirit
of mock humility, nor are we to do it in the attitude that
simply seeks to draw attention to ourselves. We are not to
do it in any other way except in order to gain the assist-
ance of the prayers of someone else. The same applies to
hearing someone else's open hearted confessions of their
own failure and sin. Alec Motyer says that we should
never do so, 'without a deliberate and single minded inten-

tion to make it a matter of prayer. Only thus will we be delivered from the spirit of prying curiosity which far from helping the needy out of his sin, would make the whole thing a matter of sin to the listener'.

Thirdly, notice the aim with which confession should be made – 'that ye may be healed'. The precise word that is translated 'healed' is used in the New Testament of both physical and spiritual healing. Let me give you an example of each. The Roman centurion's request to Jesus was 'Speak the word only, and my servant shall be healed' (Matthew 8:8), and the obvious sense is physical. But the word was used in a spiritual sense when Jesus said that part of His great mission in the world was 'to heal the broken-hearted' (Luke 4:18). There is probably a mingling of the two in James's use of the word here, although the emphasis on confession does seem to point to the spiritual. The Amplified Bible brings this out, by translating it 'that you may be healed and restored to a spiritual tone of mind and heart'. This is to be the aim of confession. If there is an instance where we feel we ought to go and speak to someone about our own problem, our own failure, our own sin; or if we know there is someone against whom we have sinned and to whom we ought to confess, let the central object of it all be that there should be healing of the spiritual situation, forgiveness, repentance, blessing, restoration of the spiritual glow, renewed usefulness in God's service. When that is the aim, then it is hardly possible to conceive of a more valuable spiritual exercise – nor of a more heart-warming demonstration of the power of prayer.

Chapter 6

ONE LAST WORD

'Brethren, if any of you do err from the truth, and one convert him;

Let him know, that he which converteth the sinner from the error of his way shall save a soul from death, and shall hide a multitude of sins.'

(James 5:19–20)

We come now to the last two verses in the whole of this Epistle. What a tremendous amount of ground James has covered since he began! – from the sovereignty of God to the use of the tongue; from the doctrine of election to the stewardship of money; from the reading of the scriptures to overcoming temptation; from prayer to criticism. Far from being a minor book in the Bible, the Epistle of James is a treasure-house of Divine truth, wonderfully spiritual and yet devastatingly practical at the same time.

Now, James comes to his last word. Some people have suggested that this ending to the Epistle is abrupt and unconnected, but it seems to me that nothing is further from the truth. These last two verses are precisely in context with the whole of the Epistle. They are the final link in a chain that stretches right back to the very first two verses where we read, 'James, a servant of God and the Lord Jesus Christ, to the twelve tribes which are scattered abroad, greeting. My brethren, count it all joy when ye fall into divers temptations'. The connection is that one word 'brethren'. He uses it in his opening sentence, he uses it another 13 times in the intervening chapters and verses, and returns to it again in his last sentence. This averages once in about every seven verses from the beginning of the letter to the end. He never seems to get very far away from this designation of those to whom he is writing. When he is teaching them, it is as brethren. When he is scolding them, it is as brethren. When he is challenging them, it is as brethren. When he is encouraging them, it is as brethren. When he is comforting them, it is as brethren. When he is instructing them, it is as brethren. It seems to me that it has not always been recognized that one of the most outstanding traits of this man that comes through in this Epistle from beginning to end in his deep, sympathetic, practical understanding and willingness to identify with the needs of the church of Jesus Christ. He writes to them in those initial verses as 'the twelve tribes scattered abroad', and then throughout the Epistle, identifies himself with them as brethren in the Lord. Do we share that kind of concern for the church of Jesus Christ? It is so easy to be critical of 'the church' and to spend a great deal of time sniping and snarling and judging and pontificating about the church in a negative and unhelpful kind of way. We need to beware of what we say about the church, especially to unconverted people. A Christian ought never to provide ammunition for the enemies of the cross. Jesus, after all, 'loved the church, and gave Himself for it' (Ephesians 5:25), and our concern should be to nourish and encourage the church in a spirit of loving concern. E. Stanley Jones once said 'I know that the church has its stupidities, and inanities and irrelevancies; but I love my mother in spite of her weaknesses and wrinkles!' We can learn from that! The church is a Divine institution, something about which we should talk with great love and concern, with which we should identify at every opportunity, and against which we should be very

careful about offering negative and unhelpful criticism.
Like his Master, James loved the church, and the whole
Epistle bears the marks of that love and concern – and not
least in these last two verses.

Turning to the text, it is interesting to notice that there
is not one imperative in the whole sentence. It is a comment and not a commandment. Yet there are no verses in
the whole Epistle that are more practical. We can discover this as we study the two main lessons they bring out.

1. *A DANGER OF WHICH WE SHOULD BE
AWARE* – 'Brethren, if any of you do err from the truth'.

To underline a point made clear in an earlier study,
notice immediately that James is speaking to Christians –
'if any of *you* do err from the truth'. He is not speaking
of people outside of the church, who have never come to
the truth in the first place. He is speaking of a danger for
Christians, and of one that has to be faced by everyone
who is a child of God. I want you to see two things about
this danger.

(1) *It is subtle* – 'if any of you do *err* from the truth'.
The Berkeley Version and the Amplified Bible translate
the word 'err' as 'strays'. In the Revised Standard Version
it is 'wanders', while J. B. Phillips paraphrases it 'wanders
away'. All of these give us the same sense, and help us
to capture the subtlety of this thing. Backsliding never
begins with a bang, it never begins with an outrageous,
scandalous sin. It always begins quietly, slowly, subtly,
insidiously. It is a wandering, a straying; not a headlong
rush into evil. It is a gradual loosening of one's spiritual
grip on life. It is not a sudden, violent jerk of the helm;
it is a slow drifting with the tide. 'If any of you strays' –
there is almost a gentleness about the word. Is it any
wonder that the New Testament teems with warnings
about this kind of danger? At least fifteen times in the
7.

New Testament we are told to 'beware'; about thirty times we are told to 'take heed'; about fifteen times we are told to 'watch'; and all of those commandments underline the same truth. In the Christian life there is no victory without vigilance. Paul says 'Therefore let anyone who thinks that he stands take heed lest he fall' (1 Corinthians 10:12 RSV). We have seen that truth earlier in this Epistle, but it needs to be underlined. No man is so far advanced along the Christian pathway, so knowledgeable in the scriptures, so experienced in Christian service, so elevated in church affairs, that he is beyond the reach of Satan, the possibility of sin, and the danger of backsliding. James says 'if *any* of you do err from the truth'. No Christian is exempt from this danger, and the first thing we must notice about it is that it is subtle.

(2) *It is serious* – 'If any of you do err *from the truth*'. No backsliding is a matter of triviality. It is all serious. When James speaks of 'the truth' here, he is speaking, of course, of the whole body of doctrine as we have it in the scriptures, and this means that it is vitally connected with every part of a man's Christian experience. It is connected with his becoming a Christian in the first place, and it is connected with his being a Christian throughout all the remainder of his life. Take the matter of becoming a Christian. Have you noticed the way in which the Bible again and again emphasizes this word, 'truth'? James himself says of God's work of salvation in our hearts that 'Of his own will begat he us with the word of truth, that we should be a kind of first-fruits of his creatures' (1:18). Paul speaks of 'the truth of the gospel' (Galatians 2:5, 14), of 'the word of the truth of the gospel' (Colossians 1:5), and of 'the word of truth, the gospel of your salvation' (Ephesians 1:13). Elsewhere, he says that we are 'chosen . . . to salvation through . . . belief of the truth'

(2 Thessalonians 2:13). We become Christians by em-
bracing the truth, by believing it, receiving it. But truth in
the Bible is not merely abstract or intellectual, it is
dynamic and moral. Normally when we speak about the
truth, we speak about something that we are called upon
to believe or to think about. When the Bible speaks of the
truth, it goes much further. This is not just something to
believe, it is something to do. We need to mark that very
carefully. Paul says that judgment comes on those who 'do
not obey the truth' (Romans 2:8). He writes to backsliding
Galatians and asks 'who hindered you from obeying the
truth?' (Galatians 5:7 RSV). The Apostle Peter com-
mends his warm-hearted and sympathetic readers for
'obeying the truth' (1 Peter 1:22). John says that if our
lives do not match up to our profession 'we lie, and do not
the truth' (1 John 1:6). Here is the same thing being repeated again and again by one New Testament writer
after another. Biblical truth is not merely to be believed,
it is to be obeyed, and nothing could be more typical of
James than that we are to be 'doers of the word, and not
hearers only' (1:22).

From all of these scriptures, and from many others,
one principle emerges: it is possible to backslide in many
ways. It is possible to backslide in the moral sphere, as
David did in the story of Bathsheba and Uriah the Hittite
for instance. It is possible to backslide in the matter of
fellowship (as it would seem some First Century Christians did in refusing to assemble together), and so deprive
the church of your contribution to its total life. It is
possible to backslide in the matter of service, to become
what Paul describes as 'weary in well doing' (Galatians
6:9), to find your life counting less and less in the thrust
and business and work of the church and its great task of
reaching the world for Christ. It is possible to backslide

in the matter of one's home life, in the biblical discharge of one's responsibilities as a parent. It is possible to backslide as a child in the matter of one's responsibility to one's parents, in the matter of honouring them and obeying them. It is possible to backslide in the deeper and inner recesses of one's own soul, to become like those of whom the Lord said 'You have abandoned the love you had at first' (Revelation 2:4 RSV), to discover slowly and sadly that you no longer have that conscious sense that the Lord Jesus is a living and precious reality to you. Yet it is probably true that every case of backsliding, without exception, begins by erring from the truth, straying from the truth, losing one's grip on the doctrines of grace and godliness.

Here is a danger of which we must all be aware. It is subtle; it is a straying, a wandering away. And it is serious, because it is a straying from God's saving and sanctifying truth. In his book on the Epistle of James, 'Faith that Works', John Bird has a section that is so excellent that, with both the author's and publishers' kind permission, I want to quote it at length. He says this –

'We are living at a time when people are saying "Doctrine does not matter. We must be tolerant to all and big-hearted enough to let all speak their minds and to hold their own opinions". Consequently, there is much confusion in the religious world. Doctrine matters greatly, for what a man believes will determine how he behaves. Our creed governs our conduct. Let a man deviate from the faith delivered unto the saints, and it will not be long before that man, morally and spiritually, strays in his ways. In the course of my ministry I have had appointments with a number of people whose lives have been marred and broken at one point or another. I have discovered that many of these, earlier in their lives, possessed an evangelical faith. They believed in the authority and inspiration of the Word of God, but at some point departed from that faith and soon lowered the standard of living and their lives caved in. When we turn aside from the doctrine of the sovereignty of God, we are soon left with no anchor and with very little assurance. We begin to question the purpose of things and lose the true perspectives of life. If we turn aside from the doctrine of the Lordship of Christ, it will not be long before we compromise our position as Christians and begin to live worldly lives. When the doctrine of sin is lost sight of, we begin to excuse ourselves for some of the things we do, and our ethical and moral standards are lowered. When the reality of the doctrine of hell is passed over and the doctrine of universalism is substituted, we miss the true meaning of Christ's death and lose any compassion we may have had for the dying souls of men. When we neglect the doctrine of the Holy Spirit, then we begin to work in the energy of the flesh and our power in service is lost. When we fail to recognize the doctrine of the meaning and function of the Church, we become sectarian and treat it as if it were a religious club. When we treat scantily the doctrine of prayer, we go to battle without any weapons, thus losing the fight against the adversary of our souls. And when we do not study the doctrine of sanctification, we become content with second-rate, mediocre, Christian living. So I may go on. We cannot gather grapes of thorns, nor figs of thistles, and we cannot expect our lives to be right if our doctrine is wrong.'

That is a clear exposition of the danger, both subtle and serious. We cannot expect our lives to be right when our doctrine is wrong. Let us beware of that, and let us guard against it by applying ourselves diligently and prayerfully to the study of the Word of God.

James now goes on to his second point –

2. A DUTY TO WHICH WE SHOULD BE ALERT –

' . . . and one convert him; Let him know, that he which converteth the sinner from the error of his way shall save a soul from death, and shall hide a multitude of sins'.

To help us understand that very long phrase, let us divide it into two sections.

(1) *The responsibility for this duty* – ' . . . and one convert him'. In the matter of the healing of a man who was sick a few verses earlier, James very clearly points out a particular responsibility belonging to the elders of the church. In the matter of the confession of sin, on the other hand, he speaks of any one of us being able to confess our sins to any other member of the Christian fellowship, within the areas we saw as being scriptural. It is this similar, more open approach that James emphasizes here. He is not speaking of the responsibility of one group of people within the church, and certainly not of the responsibility of any one man within the church. There is no hint of a special priesthood of people within the church with the responsibility, given to nobody else, of bringing people back, of 'converting' them (we shall examine the meaning of that word a little later). The point seems to be clear. The responsibility for this duty rests on every Christian in the church – though there are biblical qualifications that we shall see in a moment. Speaking of his motives and mandate for Christian service, Paul says that God has 'given to us the ministry of reconciliation' (2 Corinthians 5:18). What James is saying is that Christians are also given the ministry of *restoration*! What a precious truth that is, and how wonderfully it fits in with

other teaching in the Bible. Paul says that we are 'individually members one of another' (Romans 12:5 RSV); and that we should 'bear . . . one another's burdens, and so fulfil the law of Christ' (Galatians 6:2). The law of Christ for us, within the fellowship of the church, is a law of love. If we love each other we will have the right relationship the one to the other, for this very simple and bedrock reason, that love means that we act and speak towards a person in a way deliberately calculated to bring about their highest blessing and their deepest good. That is the meaning of love. Like so many words today, it has become perverted in the society in which we live. But to love is to aim quite deliberately for the highest blessing of the person concerned. It involves having an eager concern to do everything we possibly can for the blessing of the one who is loved. What a difference there would be in our churches if our attitude as Christians was anything approaching that today! In the context of what James is saying here, what a difference there would be in our churches if we were to have a loving and practical and pastoral concern for those we saw straying from the truth! I just sense that our hearts are such that if people are making progress in the faith, if young Christians are running well, submitting to the discipline of the church, reading the Bible, praying, attending the meetings, beginning to witness, then we find it easy to love them. Our hearts are warmed towards them. We are genuinely thrilled at the progress they are making. But if people are not making progress, if they are not submitting to the discipline of the church, if they seem to be going backwards rather than forwards, if they are being awkward rather than amenable, our attitude so often tends to be unloving and critical. Soon, we begin to neglect them, to pass them by, and as a result we miss out the very thing that James is saying here. If a person begins to wander, James infers we have a responsibility to bring him back – 'and one of you convert him'.

This responsibility strikes home in another way too, for while the Bible nowhere suggests that the work of bringing back a person who is wandering from the truth is a work exclusively given to a professional within the church, there are qualifications, which Paul gives in the Epistle to the Galatians – 'Brethren, if a man is overtaken in any trespass, *you who are spiritual* should restore him *in a spirit of gentleness*' (Galatians 6:1 RSV). There is actually another qualification in the very next sentence, because Paul adds 'Look to yourself, lest you too be tempted'. But the heart of the qualification is in those words, 'you who are spiritual'. James is saying that if a man is wandering away from the truth, the man to bring him back is the man who is himself walking in the truth. If a man is a long way from the Lord, the person to bring him back is a person who is walking closely with the Lord. We have a responsibility towards the person who is wandering away, but this carries with it a personal responsibility to guard the closeness of our own walk with God.

Before going any further let us look more closely at this word 'convert'. When we think of conversion we normally think of the moment when a person becomes a Christian. This is the sense in which Peter uses it when he calls the crowd to 'Repent . . . and be converted' (Acts 3:19), and in which Paul uses it when he says that God ' . . . now commands all men everywhere to repent' (Acts 17:30 RSV). In both cases, they are speaking of that instantaneous moment of repentance and faith. But the word 'convert' has another sense. It comes from two Greek words that would literally be translated 'to turn back', and of course that exactly fits the thought of a person who has wandered away from a direct line of truth. This seems to be the sense in which Jesus, warning Peter that Satan was going to cause him to fail temporarily in a time of crisis, added 'when thou art converted, strengthen thy brethren' (Luke 22:32). In fact, the Revised Standard Version translates it 'when you have turned again'. Jesus knew that Peter, as a natural leader, would be the special subject of Satan's attacks. He knew moreover that he would fail and deny Him – but He also knew that the day would come when he would turn back. He would be converted. He would come back into line, and walk again the pathway of obedience. In that sense we could say that every Christian 'converts' many times during his life. We can all look back on our lives and discover numberless occasions when we found that we had wandered from a direct line of truth and obedience, and the Spirit of God drew us back. There is a distinction between regeneration and conversion, although chronologically we would find it impossible to separate them. Regeneration is a sovereign work of God in which we have no part at all, that is, the bringing into being of the new birth. Conversion is something in which the awakened soul obeys and co-operates with the Holy Spirit in repenting of sin and trusting Christ. When a person becomes a Christian these two things happen. They are regenerated (a work of God in which they have no part at all) and they 'convert' (they repent and believe). Now regeneration happens once and for all. We can never be re-regenerated. We are born again, but not again and again! However, having 'converted' once, we then find that we convert again and again throughout our Christian lives. In his 'Outlines of Theology', A. A. Hodge puts it like this. 'Regeneration is a single act, complete in itself and never repeated. Conversion, as the beginning of holy living, is the commencement of a series – constant, endless and progressive.' In the case in point, James has in mind the conversion, the turning back, of a Christian from a serious drift into error of doctrine or living.

Just one last point in this section. While James uses the phrase 'and one convert him', we cannot actually convert anybody! We certainly cannot convert somebody in the sense of making them a Christian. That is beyond our power. But neither can we by ourselves restore anyone to that direct line from which they have wandered. That seems paradoxical, but there is an explanation. The point of James inferring that if a person wanders from the truth we are to convert him, is to emphasize our *personal* involvement. We are to be in this thing so completely and wholeheartedly that James can use the kind of language that would seem, on the surface, to imply that we could do the work in our own strength. There is an even more dramatic illustration of this in the story of the conversion of Onesimus, the runaway slave in the book of Philemon. Having run away, and found himself in Rome, he came into contact with Paul, who was in prison at the time, and under his influence, he came to Christ. But notice how Paul speaks of this. He says of Onesimus 'whose father I have become in my imprisonment' (Philemon 10 RSV). Now nobody in the Bible is more insistent than Paul on the sovereignty of God in the work of regeneration. Yet he says in effect '*I* have given Onesimus spiritual birth – and he uses that language to show his total involvement in the ministry of personal evangelism. Elsewhere, he even says that men will be judged 'according to *my* gospel' (Romans 2:16). Such daring language was only possible because he was utterly consumed by his message.

So here, our personal responsibility is so deep, our

involvement is to be so total, that James is able to say that we are to convert the backslider. We are to be carefully, lovingly, sympathetically watching for that wandering from the truth that begins to lead to more serious error. At the same time, we are to be careful that our own walk with the Lord is such that we are qualified to do something about it. Then, in love, and with tender concern, we are to seek to restore the wanderer to that direct line of obeying the truth that will bring glory to God and blessing to their lives; and we are to be satisfied with nothing less than that person's restoration to the fellowship and blessing of a close walk with the Lord. That is our responsibility for this duty.

(2) *The rewards of this duty* – 'shall save a soul from death, and shall hide a multitude of sins'.

James's final words are words of encouragement, just as was his first word – 'Greeting', or as it can quite properly be translated, 'Rejoice!'. He begins with a word of encouragement to those who were being oppressed and persecuted, and ends with a word of encouragement to those who were concerned about the needs of others in the Christian church – 'he which converteth the sinner from the error of his way shall save a soul from death, and shall hide a multitude of sins'.

When a backslider is converted, James says that two things are achieved, and in terms of the effort involved in this wonderful work, we can surely call them rewards.

Firstly, someone is rescued – 'shall save a soul from death'. Now for some people, this phrase indicates that a Christian can be eternally lost. The argument is this: James is speaking of a *Christian* who has erred from the truth, and if his conversion, his being brought back into a straight line, will save his soul from death, then he would *not* be saved if he did not turn. In other words, he would remain dead, and be lost for ever. That is the argument, and it seems to be logical – but it is not biblical!

Let us take a look at this issue because it does seem to be raised here, and it is of tremendous importance. Those who believe that a Christian can be lost after being saved lean very heavily on three passages of scripture, and it will be helpful to note them right away. The first is this – 'For it is impossible for those who were once enlightened, and have tasted of the heavenly gift, and were made partakers of the Holy Ghost, and have tasted the good word of God, and the powers of the world to come, if they shall fall away, to renew them again unto repentance; seeing they crucify to themselves the Son of God afresh, and put him to an open shame' (Hebrews 6:4–6). The second is as follows – 'For if we sin wilfully after that we have received the knowledge of the truth, there remaineth no more sacrifice for sins, but a certain fearful looking for of judgment and fiery indignation, which shall devour the adversaries' (Hebrews 10:26–27). The third verse is when Peter says of certain people – 'For if after they have escaped the pollutions of the world through the knowledge of the Lord and Saviour Jesus Christ, they are again entangled therein, and overcome, the latter end is worse with them than the beginning' (2 Peter 2:20).

Now those are admittedly difficult passages, and we will not have space to unravel them in detail here. But I am quite certain that they are no basis whatever for saying that when James speaks about a soul being saved from death, when a backslider is restored to a close walk with God, he is endorsing the doctrine of the possibility of being lost after being saved. Why do I say that? After all, there are those who would argue the reverse on the basis of logic. They would maintain 'James says that if

you help a wandering Christian you will save his soul
from death, which means that he would otherwise be lost
after being saved'. But look closely at those other three
passages, from Hebrews and 2 Peter. Have you ever
noticed that, in each case, the reference is to *an irreparable situation*? In Hebrews 6 we read '*it is impossible* ...
to renew them again unto repentance'; in Hebrews 10,
'there remaineth *no more sacrifice for sin* ... but a *certain*
fearful looking for of judgment'; in 2 Peter we are told
that 'the latter end *is* worse with them than the beginning'. In other words those three passages are speaking
about a situation that is absolutely beyond any kind of
reparation. There is no hope or possibility of the position
being remedied. But the whole point of what James is
saying here is that a backsliding Christian *can* be restored! That seems to make it crystal clear that those three
references cannot be married in to what James is saying.
They are obviously not speaking about the same thing.
Without arguing the case any further, we should just add
that from beginning to end the Bible teaches that every
true believer is *eternally* secure, and has what Peter calls
'an inheritance which is imperishable, undefiled and un-
fading' (1 Peter 1:4 RSV).

Then why does James say that if a person is brought
back after having backslidden his soul shall be saved from
death? There are at least two interpretations that would
fit the case. One is that James, in referring to 'death', is
speaking about the general sense of punishment for sin.
He is using this in a penal sense rather than in the sense of
utter and irreparable lostness. He is speaking of punishment for sin, both here upon earth, and in heaven in terms
of loss of reward. I must confess, however, that I find it
difficult to see why James should have used the word
'death' to describe loss of reward in heaven. On the other

hand, I can certainly see that a man, walking at a distance from God, and slipping further and further away, is missing out on so much in terms of the very essence of being a Christian, of the more abundant life that Jesus promised, that we could almost say that he is in a state of death. That is obviously a possibility.

The second interpretation is well summed up by Alec Motyer in his book 'The Tests of Faith', when he writes – 'Now, the present verses in James are not written from the point of view of what God knows about us, nor from the point of view of what we know about ourselves, but from the point of view of our fellow Christians observing our lives and hearing our talk. To them the evidence of backsliding in our lives must call in question whether we are truly Christ's or not.'

To elaborate, when James writes about a soul being saved from death, God knows that in fact the Christian never *has* to be saved from final, spiritual death, because he is eternally secure. But other people look at our lives, see us living in a certain way, and begin to call into question whether we are really converted at all. And if, following that, the word of God is brought home to our hearts, the Holy Spirit works in our lives, and some fellow Christian helps to bring us back into that live, warm, virile and happy fellowship that we once knew, then people looking from the outside would say that our soul had been saved from death. One has often heard Christians refer to a stage in their lives when some time after being truly saved, there was a period of serious regression in their lives, followed subsequently and sometimes dramatically, by a moment when they were brought back to the Lord. Sometimes, they can remember that moment as clearly as they can remember the day of their initial conversion. Looking at it from the outside, there would

be many people who would even go so far as to say that
that was the moment when their soul was saved from
death. That is the second interpretation, which would
certainly underline the one, central point being made,
namely that to restore a backslider is to rescue him from
great harm, terrible loss and serious danger. That reward
alone gives us a sufficient motive for seeking to be concerned and involved!

Secondly, someone is restored – 'and shall hide a multitude of sins', or as the Revised Standard Version puts it
– 'and will cover a multitude of sins'. The use of the word
'cover' is important here, because it brings in the atonement, the death of Christ on behalf of His people so that
a just and holy God can look favourably on the man
whose sin is covered by the blood of Christ. In terms of
justification, that is, in terms of our judicial relationship
with God, all a Christian's sins – past, present and future
– are completely, and once for all, put out of the way.
Here, incidentally, is a basis for eternal security. Becoming a Christian is not just a matter of having all of your
past sins forgiven. Becoming a Christian, being justified,
is a matter of having *all* of one's sins, past, and present,
and future, put out of the way in terms of one's eternal
reckoning with God. This is why a Christian can never be
lost once he is saved! Justification can neither be improved upon, diminished, or lost – it is once and for all,
complete, perfect and final. But in terms of sanctification,
in terms of a Christian's walk with God, there is need for
renewed forgiveness, and cleansing, a repeated need for
sins to be 'covered', and it would be consistent with our
previous point if we took this as James's meaning here.

Centuries before, David cried 'Blessed is he whose
transgression is forgiven, whose sin is covered' (Psalm
32:1). What a lovely word that is! Happy is the man

whose sin is forgiven! There is no greater blessing for the converted backslider than to have a renewed assurance that his sins are covered and forgiven, or, as Micah put it, 'cast . . . into the depths of the sea' (Micah 7:19). It was David again, in grief and remorse over his sin as a believer, who cried out 'Restore unto me the *joy* of thy salvation' (Psalm 51:12). He did not ask for his salvation to be restored – for he had never lost it! But he had lost the joy, the thrill and throb of obedient fellowship. The returning backslider can surely have no greater joy than to know that that prayer has been answered! And the Christian who is an instrument in bringing him back can share in the joy of his restoration!

So the Epistle ends on this high note – that God, in His marvellous grace, allows us as Christians to have a share in bringing about this wonderful experience in the lives of other people, by restoring to them the joy of God's salvation.

Charles Wesley has put into magnificent words the only adequate response we should gladly make, not only in our concern for wandering, wayward Christians, but in our wider concern to 'preach the gospel to every creature' –

> Enlarge, inflame, and fill my heart
> With boundless charity divine:
> So shall I all my strength exert,
> And love them with a zeal like Thine:
> And lead them to Thy open side,
> The sheep for whom their Shepherd died.